DATE DUE

NV 27 02			
NO 3 4 05			
8			
NO 16 08			

DEMCO 38-296

CHILDREN OF POVERTY

Studies on the Effects of Single Parenthood, the Feminization of Poverty, and Homelessness

edited by

STUART BRUCHEY
University of Maine

A GARLAND SERIES

HOMELESS YOUTH CREATING THEIR OWN "STREET FAMILIES"

TIA JEAN PLYMPTON

GARLAND PUBLISHING, Inc.
NEW YORK & LONDON / 1997

Library of Congress Cataloging-in-Publication Data

Plympton, Tia Jean.
  Homeless youth creating their own "street families" / Tia
Jean Plympton.
        p.   cm. — (Children of poverty)
  Abstract of thesis (Ph.D.)—University of Oregon, 1993.
  Includes bibliographical references and index.
  ISBN 0-8153-2616-5 (alk. paper)
  1. Street youth—United States—Social conditions. 2. Home-
less youth—United States—Social conditions. I. Title. II. Series.
HV1431.P59 1997
305.235'086'942—dc20   96-46671

Printed on acid-free, 250-year-life paper
Manufactured in the United States of America

Contents

Preface   *vii*
Acknowledgments   *xi*
Introduction   *3*

I   From the Library into the Streets   7
THEORY AND PRAXIS   9

II Growing Up in Western Society   11
THE CONTEMPORARY FAMILY   12
   Postmodern Descriptions   13
   Famology-Reification of the Family   15
   Multiple Models of Family   16
   Family as Action Context   17
DEVELOPMENTAL PSYCHOLOGY OF YOUTH FROM
DYSFUNCTIONAL FAMILIES   17
   The Dysfunctional Family   17
   Key Developmental Stages   20
CHALLENGES TO STREET LIFE   22
   Characteristics of Displaced Youth   22

III Methodology   29
THE STUDY SAMPLE   30
   Definitions   32
   Participants   32
   Data Collection   33

IV Getting to Know Street Youths 45
    A TYPICAL DAY IN THE STREET 45
        Interview Guide Questions 48
        Youths' Statements 49
        Case Histories 50
        Finding Historical Origins of Youths 53

V Functions of Street Families 55
    TASK-PERFORMING FUNCTIONS OF TOOLS 55
        Seeking Responsibility 57
        Developing Egalitarian Relationships 58
        Other Adults and Nonegalitarian Treatment 58
        Belonging in Your Own Turf 59
        A Place to Feel Normal 61
        Having A Recreational Unit 62
        Finding Opportunities to Contribute 63
        A Place to Teach 64
        Role Modeling 65
        Creating Personal Agency 66
        Organizing Internal and External Protocols 67
        Maintaining Family Boundaries 68
        Operating Family Discipline Styles 68
        Developing Cooperative Communication 69

VI Ritual & Mythological Features of Street Families
    REPLACEMENT BEHAVIORS 71
        Myth as a System to Bring Order to Chaos 72
        Art 73
        Origins 74
        Myths to Live By 75
        Religious Beliefs 77

VII Conclusions 81
    RECOMMENDATIONS 83
        Ending the Cycle 83

Bibliography 87
Index 95

Preface

"I think and feel like I have two faces. One face means that I can't figure out what happened to my life, what happened to have me find myself out here on the street. Also I have a face I use when I have a job to do, when I have to protect myself, a hustle to get something. That face is my fierce one, it shows how two-faced I need to be to survive."

Jere, age 15

Two-faces occurred all around me in the field during this research project. Jere, for example, clearly knows that she has more than one "face" to present. Less apparent at the beginning of this research were the multiple faces of others like social policy makers, the legal system, child advocates, politicians, as well as the general American public.

Nonetheless, the narrow purpose of this book is to draw together the words of the street youths. I talked with hundreds of participants and searched for an integrated, one-face, conceptual and strategic framework from which I could gain a researcher's perspective. But I couldn't "draw them together." On the contrary, diversity in life patterns and prospects stands out as the more prominent theme in the youths experiences.

I often got the feeling I was losing my grasp on who the street youths are. It happens when I am among them, as I was with Jere, a 15 year-old kid who had been tossed out of her home six months before. She was tortured by her biological father from about age seven.

What discourse can I have with social service workers who are overwhelmed with daily face-to-face, often fractious, contact with the angry, "fierce" face? What discourse can I have with those of the non-homeless general public who revile and judge the "worthless, won't-get-a-job street trash" who are ruining the quality of life for hard-working, taxpaying citizens?

But neither the enraged taxpayer nor the overworked and underappreciated service worker can always fully acknowledge the raw reality of homelessness beyond the grinding daily indignities.

It was going to be an elusive search for the integrated answer to "what is wrong?" The youths on the street that I know have nothing wrong with them. Theirs is more than an attitude problem reversible with more job skill training and self-esteem building projects. Any interdisciplanary approach to homelessness reveals it as a multifaceted and complex problem. Much of what researchers have described highlights who the homeless are, where they live their lives, what treatments and services they might need and how best social policy and political largesse can provide for them.

There are growing numbers and multibranching paradigms and research approaches, as well as a waxing and waning politically correct focus on the problem labeled homelessness. Each perspective adds or subtracts some empirical data and theoretical/action model to the field of study. Sociological, anthropological, epistemological, and psychological traditions frequently look for the answer. What will answer the needs of the homeless youths and other such unlucky populations? Contempt for the poor, stereotypes of low motivated groups, underclasses lacking discipline, and assorted racist, ageist, sexist assertions looking for someone to blame, are frequently offered to provide the logic for the question: "Who winds up on the street?"

But, even if each specific population of the homeless can be researched, in vivo and in vitro, this complex, historically millenniums long, social reality can't be resolved group by group in isolation from the rest of the society. Subpopulations within the youth culture are quite heterogeneous even as they overlap.

This study has modeled a "family" framework irrespective of differing racial, ethnic, and cultural backgrounds in the coding and interpreting of the raw data of youth's statements. This presumptive enforcing of a standardizing "American" view of family does limit and likely misrepresent the heterogeneity of the study's participants. Nonetheless, with this delineation of the American family, here the unit of analysis, my study did illustrate a general principle. The particular, isolated youth population explored in this study did reify the family and seek the functional equivalents that a more formal family might provide. The youths accomplished this replacement in what some view as a resource-poor street-based culture.

Therefore, this analysis offers less insight into street life—its causes and effects—than it does on the relationship between people and their ideas of what is a home. The American poet Edgar A. Guest wrote a poem that included the line, "It takes a heap o' livin' in a house t' make it a home." It was a very popular and honored poem. My interpretation of its popularity among the general American population is that a home is not the building that houses the people—but it's the relationships of the people housed within the building.

There are concrete as well as psychological obstacles in the lives of the researched youths that illustrate a piece of what it's like to be homeless—without shelter as well as nurturance. This book does neither address the central or root issues of endemic poverty, maladaptive families, nor, on the opposite end of the continuum where assignment of blame focuses, does it seek to discover individual character flaws. This research is a simple unit of analysis, not a quest for a scapegoat. The currently popular perspective of emphasizing personal responsibility lives in the political marketplace; I didn't look for it in the individual youths.

This is a human perspective of a small group of youths existing in the negative consequences of the actions of adults. The street youths told their stories to me and I coded and applied a decoding schema to illuminate a psychological model for their actions. This individual level of variable study helps to understand only one "face" at one microvariable level of this time-limited homeless period of their lives. It certainly is not my intention to explain their whole lives, let alone the phenomenon of homelessness.

In summary, the participants in this book will be helped with, and do identify, a "home" as a primary need. However, improved service delivery and more resources, a morally imperative goal, will not be enough for these many-faced youths.

Acknowledgments

I have been fortunate to have the professional and relational support of many people during the production of this book. My connection, along the way, to intellectually curious and understanding people has made this book possible.

I am ultimately indebted to all of the individuals whose world I entered and who shared their ingenious life stories with me. A notable feature of why they related so much of their culture to me is the youths' tendency to care so deeply about what happens to other citizens that share their lifestyle.

Several advisors and colleagues read all, or almost all, of the chapters in early form, and contributed ideas and criticisms that strengthened the final presentation. Judith and Michael Hibbard generously shared numerous ideas, general encouragement and never-failing patience.

As with all books, this work exists because other works came before it. This project stands on the shoulders of numerous research studies, books, formal classwork and the important connections and networks that I have enjoyed with other researchers. It was dizzying to continually transition between the twin worlds of professional academics and the professionals who work in social services, into the down-to-earth institutions, physical and social, of street life.

I believe my introduction to interpretivism and the qualitative perspectives in research was where I started to overcome my dizziness. Dianne and Philip Ferguson opened up an undiscovered opportunity for me to name and add self-discipline to a form of inquiry I had always relied upon. The research I have collected and the qualitative methods I have used to analyze it, operate from within an interpretivist world view. It has become one of the most exciting styles of research I have experienced in my professional life. I have learned from the Fergusons how to make the invisible into visible individuals who have ownership of a unique and profound social status.

I extend special thanks to Julia Hall who encouraged and motivated me. She spent hours with me as I struggled through each writer's block, was sidetracked by attractive nuisances, and fell into periods of reflective discouragement. Julia helped me get this project through all of its extended stages.

Obviously, much more could be said about all those mentioned and not mentioned above. However, no single acknowledgment could express my collective gratitude to all who helped with this attempt to honor and capture the power of those youths living in our streets.

Homeless Youths Creating Their Own "Street Families"

Introduction

LISTENING TO THE VOICES OF YOUTH

This book is about mere children. They are the youths who are perhaps lucky enough to be born into a family values era in America. But then again, perhaps they are not so lucky after all. They are the homeless youths of today's family values era who come from families that are in a crisis of inadequate child care and other social responsibilities regarding child rearing. Ann Landers polled her readers and found that 70 percent of the parents polled reported that, if they could do it all over again, they would not have children.

This book talks about young people who are fighting for their lives as they deal with issues which most Americans cannot imagine having to face at such an early age. But the fear and helplessness in the faces of these young people speak for themselves. I conducted this research because, aside from the fear, I recognized their tremendous courage and wanted others to share in their future.

Therefore, this book is an attempt to add the voices and faces of those youths into existing social science analyses. The qualitative methodology of grounded theory procedures and techniques are my chosen assurances that I will break through the inevitable biases, prejudices, and stereotypical perspectives that I bring with me to this study on street youths in their culture. The philosophical beliefs and the scientific traditions that underlie these procedures for building theory and gaining insight into the world of youths "out there," have allowed me to develop an action strategy for not distorting, yet still controlling all the masses of data, subject quotes, and reported meanings from the youths. Some of the data I discovered is quantifiable, but the analysis of what the youths portrayed is a qualitative one.

In fact, I did my best to not analyze the data, per se, too early; rather, I tried to gather and present the data in such a manner that lets the informants speak for themselves. The youths' view of their world may not match my view of reality or may not reflect "the truth." Nevertheless, the subjects' views are reported in the spontaneous and meaningful ways in which they were actually expressed. My scholarly obligation has been to hear and report what they said. I did not begin with a theory which I then sought to prove. Rather, I began with an area of study in which what was relevant to the youths was allowed to emerge.

Perhaps it can be said that my preferred adult social scientist perspectives and relevancies may not be the only reasonable ones. Adult views are not the only legitimate views. Youths have their own ideas of their culture. And who is to say objectively that one is better than the other? The point is not to decide whether youth and nonyouth claims are equally plausible. It is hard to say how much life experience is necessary before the true value of life and perhaps the relative adequacy of suicide is justifiable. The relativism of their lives sometimes will contradict traditional social analyses, values, and even modern intellectual dispositions of what should be done to their culture. They are a victimized group of mostly victimized individuals—but what else can be said about them? What non-victimizing realities do they have?

Within the youths' lives there do emerge functional traditions, brilliant folk ways and cultural leaders. These phenomena need to be appreciated. The youths are greater masters of a social world that I, the social researcher, have problems understanding and would, no doubt, negotiate very clumsily. I am clearly ignorant of what behavior is deviant, courageous, ingenious, overachieving, materialistic, trivial, provincial, or revolutionary for their social order. Which youths that I encountered were the habitués of the margins, the center, or off the continuum of the normal curve for this population?

I have sought to ask questions about the nature and social life of this youth culture which may address and consider a youth's eye view of a problem. How can members of "street families" utilize their mainstream but somewhat impoverished environment to fulfill a basic human emotional need? Is there even a basic human emotional need that they are experiencing, or have I left intact and underexamined my normal standard of "need for family?" Are families of interest to me and other social scientists because we seek to codify our cultural choices by "fixing" the youth culture? We strive so persistently to enhance their chances for opportunities to rejoin the educational and employment tracts that predominate the parent culture. But our recognition of the different cultural enterprise must beg a critical discussion. [Which culture is going to win the power struggles, for example, between assisting the youths to stay clean and sober and, perhaps, job ready, versus the youths' desire for emotional escape and recreation? Both perspectives can present heartfelt justification and principled arguments for their position.]

With that in mind, this research is not an attempt to gain the pure truth of either culture but to tell the story of a disenfranchised group in its own voices. Rather, it is very important for continued research to ask the youths themselves such questions as: "How can these no-family-nurturance conditions be changed?" By highlighting youths' experience research will gain an important perspective that will be very helpful in creating a youth-centered definition of their real life problems and the causes as they see them. If we as researchers put aside our preconceived social scientist ideas on "street families," the voices of youths may well give us new insights on emancipatory social justice that will make our analyses all the richer.

I

From the Library into the Streets

Their day begins at night when the streets are less crowded, most people have gone to their homes, and the police are less numerous. The Styth people now come out to occupy the nearly empty streets. Their guard is up nonetheless. Their appearance is remarkable: loud colors of blue, white, purple, and green heads. Some of their body adornments are bedazzling to the eye. Their gender looks indeterminate.

As a group, they seem a little like a bee society. Certain ones go to the center of the city and get into passing cars--a worker bee? Other members go inside the few open and dimly lighted buildings around--gathering sustenance or nectar? Assorted members have ingested a substance and now move as if they are in a trance-like state; others are in a frenzy. A number just seem to have disappeared into cracks and crevices in their territory. Most cities, regardless of size, report similarly behaving clans of the Styth people.

The Styth are not a foreign culture; they are, of course, street youths (with a few missing consonants and vowels). Even so, they are popularly perceived as an unfamiliar, alien, and hard-to-understand group. Their most visible and flamboyant behaviors are antithetical and threatening to many conventional American mores. These youths have no parents, do not go to school, flaunt rules and roles, have frequent sex and babies, and do not join the mainstream economy.

Does the existence of the street youth subculture challenge the premise that there is a physical, law-like relationship between elementary social behavior in a subculture and the continuing stable expression of the parent culture? That is to say, if a closer look at the youths' subculture were available, would the two cultures look more similar than dissimilar? It is a question that asks whether the homeless youth and their lifestyles are a temporary phenomenon or somehow a part of the whole culture. No post-industrial-age society has been without homeless youths. Sociologists might observe that this subculture, therefore, seems to be a stable fixture and integral component of society. Are there regularities and patterns to street culture that the sociologists of deviancy could unfold as they do when they expand on the benefits to society of various aberrant social forms?

This study is about street youths and their street family contexts. It describes one aspect of their subculture that might enliven or provide insight into the relationships between a parent culture and one of its subcultures. Regrettably, this research cannot answer all of the questions.

Street youth culture, even as a reification, exists. It is a reality that some youths leave their family homes and live on the streets in towns and cities. [When the phenomenon is studied, the research indicates multiple causes for leaving home: poor parent-child relationships, extreme family conflict, alienation from parents, interpersonal tensions, poor teacher-student relations or other school problems, physical abuse or neglect, incestuous relations with family members, and delinquency] (Adams, Gullotta & Clancy, 1985). Despite the strife and interpersonal clashes between the youths' culture and their parent culture, my research is grounded in the assumption that similarities could coexist in the two cultures. My research efforts help me better understand where to find those connections and how to understand the functions of the youths' behaviors as simply subculture specific variations of the overarching parent culture.

A primary location of these cultural connections is in the similarity of manifestations of the respective groups' family contexts. As I discovered, in the process of field work, the importance of the street family context, I went on to develop the ideas and representations of family within this context. That is, street family context was not my intended focus, but it emerged as an understanding and common aspect of the youths' lives.

THEORY AND PRAXIS

In her work with adolescent patients, Anna Freud (1958) found that they had a lower threshold for frustration, as well as a preference for action rather than verbalization of feelings, and concluded that normal adolescence is by its nature a disruption of peaceful growth, that therefore disharmony is the norm.

Having read Freud's 1958 analysis, I was beginning my data collection with my head full of sociological, anthropological, and psychological theories about youth, harmony, and parents. When I stood downtown in the plaza known to be popular with street youth, I was looking for cascades of rich data displaying sociological theories. Needless to say, the youths were not interested in me or my theoretical research. I did not explain that "theory was my goal," but I described myself as someone "interested in their lives." It was weeks later, after initial contacts that grew into conversations with a handful of youths, that I began discovering their world a tiny piece at a time.

Their spontaneous conversations and answers to my questions were piecemeal and as jumbled to me as was my understanding of their collective lives. I tried to impose typologies on the youths and their behaviors; it was too early, and I found artificial, preconceived, or mainstream relevant categories. So, I stopped and just took notes and bided my time. Eventually, my focus, the street family, emerged because of what the informants said, not because of what I thought I should find.

I was a novelty (not to mention a novice) in their culture at first, and youths were willing, some eager, to become part of my book on street youth by telling their stories. Typically, they told the story and were done with me and back to being street youths. I felt I was in their way and of no further interest. Towards the end of my days in the field, I had lost track of nearly all my early participants. A few, I knew via the grapevine, had received transitional housing benefits, an event that was great for them but reduced my encounters with them. A youth is required to be working or earnestly job-seeking while living in transitional housing.

Over the length of my time on the street, I became familiar and comfortable with the terrain. I never became comfortable with what I came to view as a very difficult and hazardous way of life. The little comfort I found in seeing how some youths gained skill and mastery in using the resources available to them was diminished by my painful awareness of how little there was available to them.

[Although each youth's story and experiences were different, the theme of heartache and peril was always predictable.]The severity of the impact of the homelessness and its personal etiology seemed insurmountable. Often, I left the field with plummeting hopes that a proper theory that will rescue these youths awaits discovery. Other times, I left the field with a better feeling after hearing a story from a youth who was feeling optimistic and hopeful that day. Even that show of faith and promise seemed a thinly veiled defense against their reality and Anna Freud's (1958) portrait of disharmony. As a balance to the perception of the youths in their individual hardships and tragedies, I also left the field and this project with the conclusion that culture, anthropomorphized into mother nature, has her own ways of taking care of society. The large body of society will continue and, in fact, the literature reveals that street youths ultimately can leave the streets. The individuals leave the streets, yet the culture stays in the streets.

II

Growing Up in Western Society

Youth constitutes a universal phenomenon. It is first of all a biological period of life, while also a uniquely human psychological unfolding. All human beings pass through various ages, and at each one they attain and use different biological and psychological capacities. At each stage the person performs the task of growing up and thereby moving on to the next stage. The tasks and roles the child performs and passes beyond develop in relation to other members of the society. My research looks to understand the relation of the subset of street youths to the social and physical manifestations of the specific subsets of families that are or were a part of their growing up.

I have reviewed three areas of the literature that I feel are relevant to the growing up processes and outcomes of the street youths in my study. The three topics are (a) the contemporary family, (b) the developmental psychology of youths from dysfunctional families, and (c) the specific lifepath risks (including HIV infection) and struggles of street youths. First, the relevant literature is used to reveal a short history covering the modern family, through the postmodern family, and ending with a current perspective of an action context for the family in Western society. Second, I discuss psychology literature which shows that a small but rapidly growing body of theories about the stages of human development is relevant. These theories consider the conditions that foster or inhibit development in children and the consequences of this early development in determining adult roles. The meaning of psychological development is not simply that new facts are accumulated or that preexisting characteristics are strengthened or weakened. What are loosely called quantitative changes in human behavior are not necessarily developmental. [Psychological development is not equivalent to physical or physiological growth. Rather, it is defined as a process of qualitative change in functioning in relationship either to the world or to oneself.] To qualify as true development, this growth must involve moving to a progressively higher level of functioning, to a new level or organization that tends to incorporate previous growth (Keniston, 1971). This developmental growth is essentially irreversible, and, at the same time, each level attained builds upon the preceding one and forms a building block for the one that follows it.

The study of psychological development during the past two decades produced startling studies of children in extreme situations of impersonal children's homes and noted a failure to develop. Such children seem never to develop the full capacities characteristic of children brought up from birth in natural or nurturant families. I have investigated the relevant literature regarding the outcomes of youths' lives when their families fail to provide basic safety and emotional) supportive environments for those crucial years of growth. Third, the literature provides both an overview and a narrow view (of HIV-risk behavior) of the challenges encountered by street youths as they struggle to achieve survival and growth on their own without the benefit of a family. This body of material follows the review of psychological development because it highlights the consequences of disrupted and immature emotional growth. The youths face a number of lifethreatening decisions and must make choices while they do not fully understand the consequences. They make choices from the psychological perspective of childlike naiveté and minimal life experiences.

THE CONTEMPORARY FAMILY

Major changes have taken place in family life over the past 30 years. Together with the likelihood of further changes before the end of the century, researchers are promoting a broad rethinking of established points of view about families and their place in society (Cheal, 1991). Postmodernism, replacing the dominant Western view of modernism, does not view the fundamental cultural shift taking place in Western societies as a process of progressive modernization. The modernists believe that the idea of progress involves tendencies toward disintegration of social forms and that this disintegration is counteracted by creative forces of reorganization. This reorganization means breaking with tradition in a progression towards more advantageous ways and forms (Berman, 1982).

The influential work of Ernest Burgess (Burgess & Locke, 1945) argues that the American family is in a state of transition from institution to companionship. In the past, he contends, a stable and secure family life was guaranteed by external controls of law, custom, and public opinion. Those controls were reinforced inside the family by the authority of the male family head, by the rigid discipline exercised by parents over their children, and by elaborate private and public rituals. That system of control broke down in America in the twentieth century, he argues (Burgess, 1926, 1973; Burgess & Locke, 1945). He believes that this disorganization is also followed eventually by reorganization.

Postmodern Descriptions

Beginning in the 1960s, the postmodern descriptions of family forms include the fact of changing family structures and add new terms and concepts. The monolithic form of family living is replaced by views of alternative lifestyles, social divisions, diversity, difference, and pluralism (Eichler, 1981). Rhona Rapoport (1989) calls the openly pluralistic approach the "diversity model." Judith Stacey (1990), for one, believes that the pluralism, disorder, and fragmentation in postmodern families are not simply the effects of a temporary phase of disorganization. She says she uses the term postmodern family "to signal the contested, ambivalent, and undecided character of contemporary gender and kinship arrangements" (Stacey, 1990). In defense of this claim, Stacey points out that the modern family system, which was based on the unity of the conjugal couple, has lost its status as both the statistical and the cultural norm. Stacey (1990) concludes that the postmodern family is not a new model of family life, not the next stage in an orderly progression of family history, but the stage when the belief in a logical progression of stages breaks down. Stacey sees the decline in productive and reproductive work in the family as the underlying cause of this period of family chaos. This structural fragility of the modern family occurs because the unity of this type of family depends on the voluntary commitments of its members, which can be redefined, weakened, broken, or abandoned, as the partners' interests change. In contrast to Stacey, Cheal (1991) posits that the family is not about to end as people are no longer perceived as interacting within sets of social relationships that they refer to as family. Rather, Cheal contends u.a. these changes mean that the family is no longer taken for granted as having one fixed form.

Feminist theorists have repeatedly challenged the assumption that there is a monolithic and singular fact (Flax, 1982; Thorne, 1982). They have emphasized both the wide variations in household composition that are found today and the findings of gender-sensitive studies of the makeup of families. Deconstructive feminist analyses of the family conclude that the family is not a concrete thing that fulfills concrete needs (Barrett & McIntosh, 1982; Collier, Rosaldo, & Yanagisako, 1982; Gittins, 1985).

Cheal's (1988) summation is that the sociological image of the family as an essential structure that fulfills necessary conditions for the reproduction of some social fact or other (e.g., society, capital, or patriarchy) has been sketched as overly deterministic.

Dorothy Smith (1993) describes the standard North American family or SNAF, as an ideological code. An ideological code, she claims, is analogous to a genetic code, reproducing its characteristic forms and order in multiple and various discursive settings. SNAF is a conception of the family as a legally married couple sharing a household. The adult male is in paid employment; his earnings provide the economic basis of the family-household. The adult female may also earn an income, but her primary responsibility is to care for husband, household, and children. The adult male and female may be parents (in whatever legal sense) of children also resident in the household. In her conclusion Smith suggests that such ideological codes may have a significant political effect by importing representational order even into the texts of those who are overtly opposed to the representations they generate.

Historically, the ideal-type family, consisting of a husband, wife, and children living together, has dominated the sociological imagination as well as social policy perspectives since the New Deal (Glazer, 1988; Lasch, 1977; Levitan, Belous, & Gallo, 1988; Scanzoni, 1983). This conjugal family has become the family, and, within this frame of reference, other family living arrangements are considered somehow deficient or not a family.

Several trends seem to signal an absolute decline in the centrality of the family, with perhaps a weakening so great that the necessary tasks it once performed will not be performed in the future. Trends in the demographic phenomena of childbearing and marriage are of critical importance to the increasing move toward "no families." (Goldscheider & Waite, 1991, p. 12)

Even when the nuclear family is not the "prevailing form," it is "the basic unit from which more complex familial forms are compounded" (Murdock, 1949). George Murdock used files containing summaries of ethnographic data accumulated by anthropologists from different parts of the world to establish the universality of the nuclear family and to declare it "always recognizable" (Murdock, 1949). Sociology reinforces this code:

The building block of nearly all human societies is the nuclear family. The populace of an American industrial city, no less than a band of hunter-gatherers in the Australian desert, is organized around this unit. In both cases, the family moves between regional communities, maintaining complex ties with primary kin by means of visits (or telephone calls and letters) and the exchange of gifts. During the day, women and children remain in the residential area while the men forage for game or its symbolic equivalent in the form of money. (Wilson, 1978, p. 553)

Famology-Reification of the Family

Famology, as a new discipline for the family field, tends to contrast the qualitative, process-orientation of the family realm with the quantitative, product-orientation of the market economy (David, 1993). Elaine David (1993) points out that such a narrow, idealistic view held by famologists will further restrict an already conservative field so that the perspective will no longer have any meaning for real-life families. J. Edwards (1989) has noted that the experiences of most families do not conform to the image of life presented by the famologists' perspective of Beutler, Burr, Bahr, and Herrin (1989). When the focus is on the positive and permanent features of family life, not only do these features tend to become culturally and historically inviolable, but the negative aspects also tend to be disregarded or labeled as perversions (Jurich, 1989; Menaghan, 1989).

Multiple Models of Family

Definitions of family need not become a delimiter of the concept where ideal-type versus perversion or no-family are pitted against each other. Gubrium and Holstein (1990) recognize that "there are innumerable contexts in which the familial is embedded." Conceiving family in a society where the family is the purported norm for everyday life is challenging. The nuclear family has what Braten (1983) calls a "model monopoly." A model monopoly results when only one perspective of a complex reality becomes universal. This narrows the range of perspectives, suppresses alternate possibilities, and makes other family forms invisible. Braten's theory is in line with the Thomas and Thomas (1928) theorem: what man defines as real is real in its consequences; that is, we can say that our concepts define what we see. Modern feminists provide an analysis that presents a new perspective on social reality and makes visible the previously invisible. Smith (1987), for example, suggests that analyses "begin where people actually are located, in that independently existing world outside of texts" because then we begin with "the particularity of an actual everyday world."

Liss (1987) says that "rather than settling for a particular definition, it seems more appropriate to define families according to the particular issues involved . . . Definitions of the family should be relative to the issue at hand rather than sacrosanct." Trost (1993) elaborates by stating he is against defining the family unless it is used as a term for a concept discussed or analyzed. In such instances, the aim of the analysis or discussion would no longer be that of a positivistic demographer's search to limit the concept.

A prevailing conceptual approach rooted in functionalist thought distinguishes the family from alternative lifestyles (Scanzoni & Marsiglio, 1993). Diverging from this old action theory, Scanzoni and Marsiglio (1993) use new action theory that assumes that persons construct their families within a social context that is both constraining and enabling. Studies during the last two decades have dealt with the alternative lifestyles. Typologies have been sorted out, and living arrangements are labeled as single parent, divorced, single, cohabiting, gay, and so on. Underlying this strategy, says Bernardes (1986), is a conceptual dichotomy between alternative lifestyles and the sociology of the family. Scanzone and Marsiglio (1993) point out that the label alternative, no matter how neutral it appears, necessarily reinforces the conceptual dichotomy between diversity and the family. Accordingly, they also point out that this dichotomy shores up the functionalist belief that the established pattern is better for society than alternatives.

Family as an Action Context

Consequently, in the process of examining this conceptual dichotomy that overlooks the dramatically changing empirical realities in Western societies, theorists are embracing one form or another of new action theory (NAT), which is about production. In this view, persons produce or create the conditions of their lives within the context of their social environment. Sometimes their environment constrains their efforts, and other times it enables their goals (Giddens, 1982). It is in NAT that the idea of the primary group is viewed as a higher order construct that can be used interchangeably with families. What emerges while using NAT is a complex image of persons exercising choice and control in a social environment that is both constraining and enabling. The youths studied in this research have been prevented from experiencing the culturally approved family. But what the youths have experienced, enables them to produce social (as opposed to blood-based or legal) families.

THE DEVELOPMENTAL PSYCHOLOGY OF YOUTHS FROM DYSFUNCTIONAL FAMILIES

The Dysfunctional Family

Street youths are displaced from unsatisfactory or dysfunctional homes. An average 60 percent of street youths have been sexually

abused in those previous homes/situations. These twin conditions
demand attention.

In the last two decades, the problem of dysfunctional families,
defined by emotional, physical, and sexual abuse, has emerged from
the cloak of social secrecy and become both a leading concern of
mental health professionals and a new topic of health research. By
definition, child abuse occurs and, in many cases, persists during
childhood. It is necessary to understand (a) how the effects of
emotional, physical, and sexual abuse are manifested at different
points in children's development; (b) how developmental factors
influence specific outcomes; and (c) how childhood experience relates
to later adjustments. Specifically, such an approach is grounded in the
field of developmental psychopathology, a perspective that examines
the evolution of psychological disturbance in the context of
development (Sroufe & Rutter, 1984). The value of this approach is
that both normative and atypical variations are considered in studying
the origins and nature of psychological disorders. Psychological
vulnerabilities in reaction to a stressful event like sexual abuse can be
conceptualized in terms of developmental factors that influence the
child's capacity to manage the stress, and in terms of specific
developmental tasks that are compromised by the stress (Cole &
Putnam, 1992).

The abuses that occur appear to emerge within a context of
broader family dysfunction. Most victims must cope with multiple
aspects of the experiences: (a) the trauma of the specific physical and
psychological events, including the violation of one's body; (b)
extended periods of apprehension, guilt, and fear between events or
assaults; and (c), the loss of a trusted relationship with the
emotionally significant person(s). Experts in the field regard the
specific effects of the pervasive, sustained stress of abuse to be most
pronounced in domains of self-development, specifically in terms of
the development of physical and psychological self-integrity and the
development of self-regulatory processes, particularly regulation of
affect and impulse control (Cole & Putnam, 1992). Moreover, the
development of self is integrally related to social development and a
sense of others; parental abuse violates the child's basic beliefs about
safety and trust in relationships, disturbing both the sense of self and
the ability to have satisfactory relationships in which one feels loved
and protected. In fact, the typical child's social supports are, in
abusive families, the source of distress.

Many studies published in psychology, psychiatry, social work,
and medical journals in the last two decades suggest an

overwhelmingly diverse range of long term effects of sexual abuse. Virtually every psychological symptom and many medical symptoms have been associated with incest, including some reported cases of no symptomology (Conte & Schuerman, 1987).

As yet, no longitudinal study has examined direct correspondences between child and adult sequelae, but similarities across samples in disturbances in the regulation of mood, self-esteem, interpersonal behavior, and impulse control are indicated (Conte & Putnam, 1992).

The developmental perspective on self and social relations states the sense of self emerges out of the transactions between the individual and others, and gains its emotional significance from the important relationships of early childhood (Bowlby, 1965). Self and social development are inextricably bound together, and dysfunction in the self domain would inevitably have its consequences in the social domain.

In current developmental psychology on attachment relationships, such attention has been given to the development of attachment (Bowlby, 1969), a construct that describes the establishment in the infant's mind of an emotionally secure relationship with the primary caregiver, typically the mother. Secure attachment in infancy leads to later childhood social competence (Waters, Wippman, & Sroufe, 1979), development of identity and self-knowledge (Cicchetti & Bughly, 1990), and the quality of adult relationships with partners and children (Main & Goldwyn, 1984).

The youths in this study typically present themselves with multiple hallmarks of the range of attachment descriptions. When they find themselves on the streets they already carry a nearly overwhelming and painful burden. The rigors and troubles of street life can be perceived to both add to and somewhat diminish that preexisting state of traumatization and despair. This study portrays some of the accommodations that youths develop to resolve their formative and pivotal attachment disruptions.

An attachment relationship is a reciprocal, anchoring, emotional and physical affiliation between a child and a caregiver (James, 1994). The child receives what is needed to live and grow through this relationship. There are three general functions that a primary attachment person provides to the child. One is protection which displays that the protector will set limits, keep the child safe and take care of it; the second is to be a provider who will supply such material things as food and shelter and the emotional basics of love, soothing, and play. The third function is one of a guide or someone who models and reflects who the child and the caregiver are and how they can fit into the world. James (1994) depicts these three functions as the building blocks of children's development, and a serious chronic lack of attachment between child and adult can negatively affect the child's growth. While there are other important developmental lines (e.g., motor, cognitive, intellectual, linguistic), attachment is the most central and essential for the survival of the infant (James, 1994).

Alterations in a child's behavior are necessary for its survival when the three functions are not met by a primary attachment. The alterations in a child's behavior are attempts to maintain attachment relationships at almost any cost. The child can suppress spontaneous thoughts, feelings, and wishes and, instead, play adaptive roles in order to stimulate caregiving behavior in the adults or parents. Such children's adaptive roles include being overly compliant with abusive parents, being entertainers with distracted parents, being mini-caregivers with needy parents, being demanding bullies with nonresponsive parents, or being manipulators with neglectful, withholding parents (James, 1994). When these children's parents respond to the adaptive roles being played out, a chain of events is begun. The youth notes an association between their inauthentic role and a responsive caregiver. These children do not have the experience to perceive these as maladaptive or manipulative relationships; instead, they perform what is necessary to find some level of attachment. Here the child's worthiness will be anchored in the role developed to compensate for an inadequate attachment relationship.

When a child experiences a violent, neglectful, or malappropriate home life attachment, disturbances can result because the child believes the adult cannot protect it. Other attachment caregivers are sought to provide the power and strength that are necessary to fulfill the three functions of attachment. For such support the youngsters often turn to peer groups (James, 1994).

Key Developmental Stages

Developmentally, during infancy and toddlerhood, the infant is very dependent on adult caregivers and, in sum, during these stages there are significant advances in the development of a sense of self, of initial self-regulatory functions, and of trust and sensitivity in social relations. In the case of abusive parents/caregivers, the infant's basic sense of physical integrity of a separate self, basic trust in the responsive love and protection of the parent, and sense of control over events are threatened.

During preschool years, in terms of social and self-development, the child's task is to learn to integrate his/her secure sense of agentic self with the restrictions of the social world. Preschool age self-regulatory behavior includes setting limits on one's own behavior (Kopp, 1982), cooperating with others (Hartup, 1983), and being accountable for rule violations (Dunn, 1988). Preschoolers are aware of basic rules of social roles and are distressed when rules are violated (Kagan, 1981). Sexual abuse at this age compromises the ongoing self-organization and self regulation that are major tasks of the period and sabotages the earlier accomplishments of infancy and toddlerhood.

In the elementary school years that precede the onset of puberty, the social and self-developmental tasks revolve around an increasing sense of cognitive and social competence and control (Connell, 1990). Abuse at home at this age challenges the likelihood of the victim's ability to increase the scope of social experience and to establish a sense of self-competence in the social world beyond the home. Intense guilt, shame, and confusion diminish the likelihood of feeling secure enough to build friendships and to receive social support. Unable to relate realistically to emotionally intense experiences and lacking an adequate model of flexible self-control in the home, the child may exhibit undercontrolled behavior or may vary between rigid and poor control. Although denial and dissociation usually decrease during this period, they appear to remain elevated in sexually abused children (Adams-Tucker, 1985).

The most salient aspect of the developmental changes of adolescence is the onset of puberty and emerging sexuality. The psychological task of identity formation (Erikson, 1968) requires the adolescent to integrate the complex and self related features and consolidate them into a unified, continuous sense of self that is compatible with the self-view and the view of others. Most adolescents report harmonious relationships with their parents and seek their parents for guidance about important decisions (Josselson, 1980). Adolescents' continuing developmental tasks of integrating the multiple and changing aspects of self are significantly jeopardized if the victims of abuse had to rely on coping through denial and dissociation; therefore, the risk for psychopathology is heightened. Reliance on relatively immature coping strategies which preempt reflection, reasoning, and planning, increases the likelihood of adolescents acting impulsively when frustrated, depressed, or anxious.

Typically, these adolescents engage in misconduct, such as substance abuse, sexual acting out, running away, and other self-destructive behaviors.

To summarize, childhood abuse interferes with typical self and social development, and the disorders most closely associated with a childhood of abuse reflect these impairments in self and social functioning (Cole & Putnam, 1992). Research in developmental psychology reveals that self development and social development are important continuing themes throughout infancy, childhood, adolescence, and adulthood and that each developmental transition is associated with revision and change in one's self-definition and integration, in the self regulation of behavior and affect, and in the scope and quality of one's social relationships. Any social services conceptualized for displaced youths could benefit from the illustration of how many developmental transitions, independent from their physical age and educational pathways, they have yet to achieve.

CHALLENGES OF STREET LIFE

Characteristics of Displaced Youth

The label homeless suggests that an individual's problems will end with the provision of housing. Homeless youths do need housing, but they also have a complex assortment of other acute problems, including a lack of employment skills and a lack of the basic necessities (clothing, food, health care, etc.) that are often otherwise provided by the youth's family. Additionally, labeling youths homeless only adds to their negative self-image and deters many youths from seeking assistance from agencies associated with homeless services. I will use the term displaced youth or street youth to describe persons under the age of 19 who have no viable family or community housing resources or who are living in unsafe or unstable environments. Many of these youths, while visible on the streets, do have access to shelters. Nonetheless, the streets are their homes and the source of all that an ideal home would otherwise provide economically, emotionally, psychologically, culturally, and spiritually.

Displaced youths include those who have left their homes without a parent's or guardian's consent (runaways), those who are thrown out of their homes (throwaways), those who have problematic social service placements (system kids), and those lacking basic shelter (street youths). Approximately 21 percent of youths seeking emergency shelter are throwaways and on their own (GAO, 1989). Because adolescents are often barred from welfare hotels, youths often become throwaways or systems kids when their parents become homeless (CDF, 1988). Runaways living in shelters are typically younger and more likely to be female than are those youths living on the streets (GAO, 1989). About half of runaway youths are also system kids. having spent some time in the foster care system (Robertson, 1989), and nearly 12 percent of all displaced youths have left foster care or a group home immediately before seeking public shelter (GAO, 1989). Thus, the distinctions between runaways, street youths, throwaways, and systems kids are often unclear, as the groups frequently overlap.

National estimates of the number of displaced youths aged 11 to 18 have increased from 519,000 in 1975 to 1.5 million in 1988 (CDF, 1988). Contrary to portrayals in the popular press, most displaced youths are not transient but come from the local community (Chelimsky, 1982). As with homeless adults, the ethnicity of street youths typically reflects the ethnic breakdown of their local geographic community (GAO, 1989). Nationally, the majority of displaced youths are Caucasian and do not receive public assistance. In large urban centers such as New York City, however, most displaced youths are poor and are black or Hispanic (Shaffer & Caton, 1984).

Displaced youths are more likely than non-homeless youths to have no parental figures available or to come from single parent families (GAO, 1989). Also, their families are typically the source of the greatest stress rather than support. Street youths have limited alternatives for housing (Institute of Medicine, 1988). In 1974, a national network of short-term residential shelters was established and designed to serve approximately 300,000 youths per year. However, over the last ten years, the demands for shelter have increased, and the resources have decreased (GAO, 1989). Many adolescents turn to temporary situations such as living with friends. The majority who leave foster care or a group home placement do not return to their original living situation after receiving shelter. Even in shelters, youths are rarely provided with comprehensive services, and daily life is difficult. Hunger, incidents of physical and sexual assault, robbery and burglary, and undiagnosed and untreated medical and emotional problems are widely documented for these youths. Approximately half

are not enrolled in school, and about half of those in school have
learning or conduct problems (Egan, 1988). Displaced youths are at
high risk for suicide, approximately one third having attempted
suicide (Robertson, 1989). Depression frequencies range from 26
percent to 84 percent (Robertson, 1989). The lack of supportive
resources and the existence of multiple problem behaviors and
emotional distress must be considered in the design, implementation,
and evaluation of HIV-related services for displaced youth. As one
adolescent in a shelter expressed the problem: "Why should I care
about dying ten years from now when I do not know where I will
sleep and how I will get food tomorrow?" (Rotheram-Borus &
Koopman, 1991). The risk of HIV infection can be addressed only in
the context of the youths' lives.

The risk of AIDS infection is increasing among displaced youths
in the United States. The HIV epidemic is currently spreading most
rapidly among the disenfranchised and those least able to protect
themselves and to secure medical services (Luna, 1991). There are
about 1.5 million homeless adolescents, approximately 4 percent of
whom are estimated to be infected with the human immunodeficiency
virus (Stricof, Novick, & Kennedy, 1991). These approximately
60,000 teenagers are infected at a rate of 2 to 10 times higher than the
rate reported for non-homeless agemates (St. Louis et al., 1989). This
high rate of infection can be expected to rise higher, in part because
the social networks of this group have a high rate of seroprevalence
(the prevalence of subjects whose serological test for the presence of
HIV antibodies has converted from negative to positive) (Hein, 1989).

Homeless youths engage in sexual and substance abuse behaviors
that place them at increased risk of contracting HIV, and they
demonstrate other problem behaviors that reduce their coping
responses. As a group, their profile reflects youths who have been
thrown out of dysfunctional families or have run away to escape
victimization and neglect. They have difficulty satisfying basic needs
for shelter, food, and health care; to survive economically, displaced
youths live in undesirable neighborhoods that have high rates of HIV
prevalence (Penbridge, Yates, David, & MacKenzie, 1990). The
resulting stress and consequent problem behaviors yield many health
risks, and HIV infection is only one.

Existing seroprevalence data suggest that about 4 percent of
displaced youths are already infected with HIV, with the rates varying
across cities from 2.1 percent in Houston to 5.3 percent in New York
City (Stricof et al., 1991). These high rates exist despite survey data
that indicate that displaced adolescents are as well informed and

motivated to prevent HIV infection as are their non-homeless peers (Goodman & Cohall, 1989). However, studies also indicate that knowledge of AIDS is not enough motivation to maintain safe behaviors (DesJarlais & Friedman, 1988). To explain the high seroprevalence rates among displaced youth, the living situations and specific HIV risk acts, such as unprotected sexual acts, must be examined.

Displaced youths gravitate to places where they are most likely to find HIV positive sex partners and to be introduced to IV drug use. Such places also provide resources for economic survival, bartering sex and selling drugs, which are obvious avenues of potential HIV transmission. About one quarter of displaced youths in Los Angeles and New York City report trading sex for money or drugs (Rotheram-Borus & Koopman, 1991). Boys who engage in sexual activity in exchange for money or drugs typically do so with same-sex partners, even those who identify themselves as heterosexual. Adults in the youths' social network also survive through drug dealing and working in the sex industry. In such an environment, atypical behavior appears normative, and the risk of HIV infection may increase substantially. This situation exists in most large urban centers, so that the HIV seroprevalence rate in social networks of street youths is unusually high.

Sexual risk behaviors are more common among displaced than among non-homeless adolescents. Although similar percentages of both adolescent groups engage in sexual activity and similar percentages use condoms (Goodman & Cohall, 1989), almost 50 percent of displaced males have had more than 10 sexual partners in their lifetimes, compared with less than 7 percent of adolescent males nationally (Turner, Miller, & Moses, 1989). Pregnancy and teenage motherhood are higher among displaced youth compared with non-homeless youths (AMA, 1989). Between 50 and 71 percent of street youths have a sexually transmitted disease (Shalwitz, Goulant, Dunnigan, & Flannery, 1990). During the three months before seeking shelter, the typical boy has four or five sexual partners, and the typical displaced girl has one or two partners (Rotheram-Borus & Koopman, 1991).

The risk of HIV transmission through IV drug use varies dramatically by neighborhood, although the rates are consistently higher than among non-homeless adolescents (CDC, 1988). In addition, frequent use of alcohol and non IV-drugs places displaced youths at risk for HIV by disinhibiting sexual risk behaviors.

There are three subgroups of displaced youths at particular risk for HIV. First, about 6 percent of street adolescents identify themselves as gay or lesbian (National NRYS, 1991). Gay male adolescents are likely to engage in sexual activity with gay men, who as a group have the highest known seroprevalence rate in the United States, and to begin sexual activity at an early age (Rotheram-Borus & Koopman, 1991). Second, as many as 60 percent of displaced youths report being sexually abused (Barden, 1990). Sexual abuse often forces youths to leave home, and it is also associated with having greater numbers of sexual partners, which increases the risk of HIV infection (Rotheram-Borus & Koopman, 1991). Third, 39 percent of displaced youth currently meet criteria for a diagnosis of drug abuse, a rate five times higher than that of non-homeless youth. These data present a consistent picture, revealing that street youths are at high risk for H[V infection. The risk emerges not only from their own sexual behaviors and substance abuse but from their concentration in neighborhoods with the highest seroprevalence rates. HIV is, however, not the only potential risk factor in the lives of most displaced youth.

Summary:
Youth occupy a marginal status in our society, and anyone in a marginal position typically experiences some measure of anxiety. Irving Sarnoff (1962) describes the marginality of youth:

> In our society . . . the adolescent is generally obliged to live for many years as a marginal man . . . That is, his social status is rather ambiguous, for he is considered neither an adult, nor yet a child; neither permitted to share the prerogatives of adults nor enjoy the irresponsibility of prepubescent childhood; neither taken completely seriously by adults nor ignored by them as they might ignore the antics of a young child. (p. 392)

An overwhelming set of tasks for street youths is a consequence of the general tension created by the uncertainty of living on the street. My research to understand how youths survive and grow up with these anxieties could not be separated from the triple understandings of their early developmental history, the general meanings of contemporary families, and the challenges of the youths' street subculture.

Street youth culture, more properly subculture, is neither clearly separated from the parent culture conventions nor unified within itself.

Why is this youth subculture not so separate from the parent culture? Do the youths, who in the past have been a part of a family, now look forward to reentry into a conventional life? My search for such substantive theories (i.e., what is the nature of street families?) is the search for building blocks for a formal theory. A fuller understanding of what the mechanisms of cultural transmission are can help.

III

Methodology

The focus of this research is to investigate and describe the culture of life on the streets for youths who have been displaced from their homes. This is to be applied research with a goal of producing substantive theory. It is looking at a human problem and is intended to contribute knowledge that will help people understand the situation of displaced youths. The key assumption in this research is that the existence of this culture and its definition as a social problem can be understood and solved with knowledge. My purpose is to add to that knowledge. I have chosen to conduct an ethnography because of its capacity to depict the activities and perspectives of the actors. From their own perspective, the dangerously misleading preconceptions that social scientists often bring to research can be challenged. The culture of street youths is especially vulnerable because it is not easily accessible and is easily misunderstood.

Since ethnography does not entail extensive pre-fieldwork design, the strategy and even direction of my research was changed relatively easily (Hammersley & Atkinson, 1987). The description of the youths' culture was the primary goal. I was looking for detailed descriptions of the concrete experiences of life on the streets and of the social rules and patterns that constitute it. This methodology discouraged me from the temptation to discover oversimplified models of their complex lives.

My original focus changed as a result of my evolving perspectives and ongoing assessments. What was a provisional category or what was a developing interest in naturalist research is viewed as a step in the process towards a denser and thicker description. The focus on the street family emerged after a few months of general data gathering in the field. Over time, this focus narrowed into one on the street family as a context.

Although the street family is mentioned in the relevant literature, detailed knowledge is absent. In grounded theory this is a "foreshadowed problem" and the phenomenon of the problem becomes a starting point in research (MacIntyre, 1977). During the course of the fieldwork, I identified a number of issues within the street family with more precision and developed the category. Eventually, these local manifestations of my category and ideas can next be compared in other fields and studies and generalized beyond my topical interest.

The research was a reflexive process operating throughout every step of the project. I recognize that I am part of the social world under study (Hammersley & Atkinson, 1987) and that as such, reflexivity must be a part of what I study and how I bring my common sense knowledge and common sense methods into my investigation. I worked with my reactivity in the field by incorporating into my field notes my reactions, the youths' reactions to me, and the interactions of both subjective experiences. How we all responded to each other was considered information to consider in other situations or patterns I saw in the youths' lives.

THE STUDY SAMPLE

The participants for this study were found in the street institutions that surround their lives. The youth do move between street institutions and conventional institutions (such as parental homes, group homes, and agency placements); however, all contacts for this study were made on the streets. These contacts were typically in parks, downtown outdoor plazas, youth-oriented cafes, perimeters and lobbies of agencies serving displaced youth, and other such places. Several organizational characteristics influenced the nature of this sample.

1. These are all downtown area contacts within a city whose housed population is about 500,000. This core of central city

displaced youth is approximately 80 youths per night. The total population of displaced youths in the urban and suburban area is about 2,000 per year. The downtown population of youths is less isolated than other displaced youths who avoid the downtown youth culture and its specialized organizational structures.

2. These downtown youths are predominantly white. There is a smaller proportion of youth of color in this population than in the population of the city.

3. The downtown area has a district with gay-oriented business and clientele that appeals to gay and lesbian youth and offers them some social acceptance. The combined effect of rejection from home and attraction to downtown has resulted in a higher than usual concentration of gay, lesbian and bisexual youth in this sample.

Study participants were volunteers and thus, by definition, self-selected. There is no way of knowing whether youth selected themselves as participants due to their relative dissatisfaction with their street life or their relative comfort and hope for discussing their situations with an outsider. In any event, those who selected themselves as participants may well have differed from those who did not make my prearranged meetings and follow-ups or who refused to talk because of their unwillingness to trust outsiders.

About 30 youths were contacted during the early stage of entering the field, which included the months of November and December. There were 16 youths involved in talks and interviews during the December through May period of data gathering, which focused on the street family. In stage two, where street family became street family context, I interviewed five youths by using the interview guide. Finally, in March and April, I interviewed five individuals for more data and assurance that the earlier data were not atypical.

There were no key informants. The youths do not lead predictable lives and additionally had no phones. Approximately one-third of the follow-up or second interview arrangements were kept. Most contacts with the youths occurred because I knew and frequented their hang-outs. Overall, I talked with over 100 youths either singly or in groups. I wrote field notes on fifty-five individual events. These events were contacts lasting from a few minutes to about one hour.

Definitions

Three criteria were used to determine a participant's inclusion in the study. First, a participant had to have been involved in leaving the home of the family of origin (birth parents) or of a legal guardian. This act of leaving, voluntarily or involuntarily, had to result in a period of time when the youth was living unsupervised by a responsible adult. This definition of displaced youth is insensitive to when the youth first began to leave home, how many times the youth returned to home, or was intermittently housed or institutionalized by authorities. In other words, the length of time in the street life and, to a certain extent, the youth's current housing or shelter circumstance were not used as exclusionary determinants. This is a transient population. Also, a group of youth on the street, at the plaza, or in a cafe is often a blend of youth without a home, former homeless youth, and those characterized as weekend warriors (youths who run away from home only on weekends). Second, a participant had to have first left home before reaching 18 years of age. Formerly on-the-street youths, of up to the approximate age of 22 do maintain contacts with their still-in-the-street-life friends. I included their comments; however, none became primary participants. Third, a participant could be female, male, or self-identified cross-gender individuals. Additional criteria involving the relationship of the displaced youth to the members of the left-behind family, the nature of those current family relations, and so forth, were avoided.

Participants

As is often the case in exploratory research, the selection procedures for this study were based on purposive rather than random sampling (Mayer & Greenwood, 1980). Although dysfunctional families and abuse within those families have been described as relentlessly democratic (it happens across all socioeconomic statues), the study participants need not display an even distribution of demographic variables. As with other studies on similar disenfranchised populations, the participants were neither randomly drawn nor representative. In fact, many of the participants are from the local area (United States Pacific Northwest), with minimal travel to or from other states. Findings from such a select group in a city of medium size clearly may not apply to other groups of displaced youth. Unsound extrapolation may occur if the readers do not remain aware throughout of the nature of the sample. Unsound interpretation may likewise occur. For example, youths of color are very much underrepresented, and youths of sexual preferences other than heterosexuality are very much overrepresented. I often used snowball sampling with these youths. The reader should obviously not conclude from this ethnographic study that displaced youths are in almost every instance white. Neither should the reader conclude that displaced youths are often non heterosexual.

No attempt was made to obtain a large sample. Since the intent of an ethnographic study is to inquire about the properties of a given phenomenon, not the frequency or the distribution of those properties, sample size is a relatively unimportant matter in exploratory research (Mayer & Greenwood, 1980). In this particular study, the participants were purposely limited in number (though arduously secured) in order to provide sufficient data to undergo in-depth analysis without research becoming unmanageable, prohibitively time-consuming, or less focused than desired. Likewise, there was a limit to the time available for generating data. This process was in keeping with the objective of the research, which was, as with all qualitative research, to present "the vividness of 'what it is like' with an appropriate degree of economy and clarity" (Lofland, 1971).

Another factor to mention briefly is bias. The reader should remain aware throughout that the author is a woman from a dysfunctional family of origin. The very same attributes that assisted the research design, collection, and analysis are also potential sources of bias, as is the author's feminist perspective. The study findings should be considered accordingly.

Data Collection

There were approximately three stages of data collection: stage one was entering the field and occurred from November 1992 through January 1993; stage two, choosing a focus, was from January 1993 through March 1993; and stage three, refining the focus, was from March 1993 through May 1993. Each stage contained data for its stated purpose as well as applicable data for the next purpose.

Therefore, data sometime became less applicable though not obsolete. Data built on data.

My work in the field began in November, 1992, and ended in May, 1993. During those seven months, I achieved three consecutive objectives: (1) to gain entrance into the culture and to become familiar with the youths in their culture, (2) to choose a focus for the study, and (3) to develop and refine that focus. Each of these objectives occurred in a sequence that loosely could be labeled stages of the study.

Stage one began in November when I first entered the areas where I'd heard youths liked to hang out. While stage one eventually was followed by stage two activities, I never stopped gaining familiarity with the youths and their culture. Early stage one (November and December) was the time period that yielded the longest data sets. A data set is the collected pages of notes written from one field contact and does not depend on time elapsed or number of youths contacted in that field contact. A period of 30 to 40 minutes observing and participating in the field would yield an average of six to ten pages of field notes. These notes typically recorded what I saw, overheard, or felt while I was in the streets, parks, etc. My conversations with the youths, this early, were often as brief as one sentence or syllable to a few minutes. The brief conversations continued throughout the length of my seven months in the field. Conversations with the youths became more comfortable and grew longer as my familiarity with the streets increased. I had one-to-one contact with 30 youths and wrote 26 data sets from this stage, covering November 1992 through March 1993. These data sets contain an average of six to twelve direct quotations from the youths. Overall, I was able to have longer (i.e. 30 minutes) contacts with 15 different youths and these became the source of my data sets classified as interviews.

As part of stage two, beginning in the March fieldwork, my objective was to finalize a focus for the study. I has been collecting data and using open coding processes for analysis in stage one. I continued this process during stage two and added axial coding to the coded data.

The addition of axial coding allowed me to begin simultaneously to reduce the amount of data I worked with and to close up the data. The fullest range of data that I had opened up previously contained many foci and categories that this research could not consider. The narrowed focus on street family was put together in relationships containing the concepts that I had previously coded out in open coding or just recently coded in response to the new focus.

I had contact with about 60 youths during this three-month period and recorded 19 data sets from those contacts. Most were unduplicated contacts. Three youths met me at two separate settings and thus yielded six of the 19 data sets. Data sets began to contain less of the more global observations of "everything I saw" and to contain specific material pertaining to the street family context. To keep focused, I relied on the interview guide and questions. Nonetheless, I was continuing to evolve and improve the questions on my guide sheet. Most interviews during this stage transpired in the restaurants the youth would choose and at the time that they decided.

Finally, in stage three, I refined the concepts in the focus. The axial coding process allowed me to complete the development and increase the density of subcategories with their properties and dimensions. I considered this process to be the key and pivotal accomplishment of the study. During this period (March through May) the concepts were brought to life and the understanding of the street family concept became an model or paradigm in grounded theory.

A good, grounded theory will be comprehensible to the informants and to an outsider reading my theoretical story line with its social science emphasis. Therefore, guided by my building concepts and focused questions, I went back and forth between the early data and the newer material. After I verified compatibility between my story and the youths' stories, I felt I was done and could leave the streets.

To refine the focus, I had contacted 20 youths during this stage. I recorded ten data sets from those contacts and noted that seven of those youths were newly found informants for my study. These last data sets were sometimes one or two pages in length. These pages contained essentially verbatim quotations from the youths.

In summation, I recorded 55 data sets. I had close contact with about 110 youths and had casual contact with about twice that many. Participants were encountered on their turf or in the streets they traveled, in cafes and businesses they favored, in public areas they had claimed, and in social service agencies where they were welcome. I started the majority of conversations with the youths. Sometimes I explained my researcher status early, although after awhile (weeks later) many knew what I was doing on their turf.

The issue of the rationale for the study was never challenged; my assurance of confidentiality was of minor concern; and many youth lost or tossed their copy of the informed consent I reviewed and left with them. I kept the signed consent form and would hand the youths an unsigned copy that stated their rights and privileges and contained my contact phone number. One youth used that contact number to invite me to a coffee meeting. No tape recordings of the interviews were made.

Throughout the study, I assumed the role of observer-participant, a technique most often used in ethnographic studies of different cultural groups. More than a questioner or passive observer, I participated in some topics being studied. I shared some of my stories with the youths, and they shared theirs with me, thereby equalizing the power associated with nondisclosure. This approach is consistent with a feminist research paradigm, "locating both researcher and researched on the same critical plane" (Coyner, 1988-1989, p. 291). R. K. Yin (1984) strongly argues for the value of this approach to data collection, in terms of accurately perceiving reality from the viewpoint of the person(s) inside the study.

I conducted the interviews in an open-ended style, initiating discussion with a single interview question: "I'd like you to tell me about your street life." The design of the focused interview guide followed the development of Merton, Fiske, and Kendall (Sjoberg & Nett, 1968). It is typically used with individuals known to have been involved in a particular experience when the researcher has already previously analyzed that experience. The focused interviews allowed me to explore in greater depth data on the street family concept previously generated. These interviews were focused on the subjective experiences of the youths, with the objective being to understand the personal meaning given to the experience by each youth.

In keeping with this objective, I avoided influencing the youths' direction or prioritizing of areas under investigation. Based on early analysis of the first interviews, an interview guide rather than a structured protocol was prepared for the interviews. This interview guide was consulted to ensure that key topics were covered in the interviews. These topics were inquired after if they were not addressed in the whole of the interviewee's spontaneous response. The open-ended style of the interview permitted the youth to disclose information in their own manner and time.

The interviews lasted anywhere from five minutes to one hour. The majority were less than one-half hour. After the interview, I wrote process notes as soon as possible. These were to record impressions, observations, and as-accurate as-possible quotations from the interviewees. I also reminded the youth of my availability and contact telephone number in case the interview experience had become uncomfortable after I left and the youth, therefore, wanted an appropriate referral. No youth ever called for a referral.

Data Analysis

The material to be analyzed was from the interviews and field notes. Unguided interviews at the start of the project underwent qualitative analysis with three objectives in mind. The first was to identify emerging patterns and themes. The second was to discover the range of variation within the early contacts with respect to general street life. in part for the purpose of planning further interview strategies. The third objective was to generate an interview guide based upon the early data.

Analysis was an ongoing reflexive process, beginning with the exposure and observations during early field presence. Data were informally analyzed and tentatively organized throughout the period during early exposure in the streets (November through December 1992). I was using open coding during this stage. Insight and understanding gained at each stage of the exploratory research were integrated into subsequent stages and analysis and were continually refined. Analysis of the early interviews was based upon and adapted from the method of qualitative analysis described by Lofland (1971). Themes identified in the analysis of the early conversations were those apparent in the statements of the youth.

> Participants under study are themselves analytic. They order and pattern their views and their activities . . . In order to capture the participants "in their own terms" one must learn their analytic ordering of the world and their categories for rendering explicable and coherent the flux of raw reality. That, indeed, is the first principle of qualitative analysis. (Lofland, 1971, p. 7)

Early on in the field, the statements of the youths were clumped, as a few themes and patterns began to show up with some consistency. Thus, inductively generated categories emerged. This body of data from youth interviews did not articulate sufficient indigenous concepts regarding the street family, so I chose to develop sensitizing concepts. These sensitizing concepts, which have their origins in social science theory or the research literature, gave me "a general sense of reference" and provided "directions along which to look" (Blumer, 1969). I used the application of sensitizing concepts to examine patterns of the street family and how it is manifest for the street youths.

The street phrase "don't rat" is understood by street youths and the personnel who work with them as a law of the street culture. It is usually explained as a rule that is essential to survival. I developed a sensitizing concept when I reconciled the two street rules "don't rat" and "survival first" as one maxim.

I first had to wonder which rule was the higher order rule and how each youth sorted these two out. These were two absolutes in conflict with each other and my conventional, non-street-based logic and experience were inadequate. Clearly, more research needs to be done into the, "to whom, for what reason, when, where, and why can you rat?" Nonetheless, my newly sensitized consciousness toward street culture allowed me to keep seeking subjective perspectives rather than an objective reality.

Axial Coding

After sufficient data and early sensitizing concepts began to emerge in the first stage of the study, I began to apply axial coding methods in the grounded theory tradition of qualitative research. Strauss and Corbin (1990) define axial coding as a set of procedures whereby data are put back together in new ways, after open coding, by making connections between categories. This process is done by using a coding paradigm involving conditions, context, action/interactional strategies, and consequences. The development of a story line is the important beginning in grounded theory according to Strauss and Corbin (1990). This general descriptive overview is restricted to the main problem and question. Lesser problems are developed into story lines also; however, the main story line allows the focus of the research to develop within integrated categories, often of lesser categories and story lines. The main story line for my research goes like this:

This story is about how displaced youths accommodate to the loss of what the former families ideally would have provided. Youths attempting to accommodate can only marshal the tools and abilities they perceive and apply them to the available resources that they can perceive.

An accommodation that some youths exhibit is their attempt (to reduce the frustration and anxiety) to compensate for those losses they feel. One not necessarily conscious compensation strategy is to replace certain lost functions or features of the family. These youths, again not always with a clear purpose to replace, participate in the street family context. Within this reified street family context, the youths experience a range of satisfaction with their replacements.

This overview story line contains six elemental units central to the axial coding process for data analysis. For this study, the keys are: (a) causal conditions, loss of functional family; (b) phenomenon or event, accommodating to the loss; (c) context, personal tools needed for accommodating behaviors; (d) intervening conditions, external resources available; (e) action taken, replacement strategies of participating in street family context; and (f) consequences, the range of successes at replacing what is lost. Each of these six key units is explained in the following pages.

Each of these six units is called a category, and each has a number of properties that are attributes or characteristics pertaining to their category. Also, properties have dimensions, or locations and degrees of properties along a continuum. It is the relationship among these categories, their properties and dimensions, that build the model or concept that becomes the understanding of what is being studied.

Causal Conditions

During the beginning of each analysis of an event, the first consideration listed is the causal condition or antecedent. This research considers the causal condition to be the loss of a functional family, including its basic functions and services. The loss of such family functions does not necessarily lead any single youth to leave a family home. Nor do the types and/or degrees of the loss create a specific threshold of severity that all street youths experience. My concept to lose a)family does not always mean to become homeless or to join the street culture. At home youths experience many of the same losses when they live in a dysfunctional family.

One set of properties for this category of loss is the list of which family functions are now missing for the youths. The youths do not always have the ability to articulate the losses, and the losses are sometimes simply felt as an emptiness or unnamed anxiety. The list of ideal or normative family functions continues to be an elusive political and practical category in the social sciences. Even so, there is an intricate pattern of human needs. How growing, maturing youths fare without certain critical features or family functions is a complex question. My study did not focus on the losses of material goods and services; rather, my focus was on the psychological or nurturant realm of losses.

Phenomenon

The central idea in the story line is the phenomenon or event towards which the action strategies are directed. This study is about how the youths choose to accommodate the loss of a functioning family. The properties and dimensions of the youths' accommodation choices and behaviors begin to make the analysis complex and more reflective of real life. This basic model is the framework waiting for the details to give it density. One of the decisions to be made by the youths is the choice to leave home. The existence of a dysfunctional family needs to be accommodated for by at-home youths, as well as by institutionalized youths, by part-time at-home youths, and, of course, by street youths.

Classical psychological accommodations that people choose when faced with loss can include mental deterioration, delinquent or acting out behaviors, suicide, depression, hyperactivity, decompensation (loss of ability to cope), and, of course, the full set of happier choices, such as gaining maturity and flexibility. Some street youths have been literally kicked out of their homes; others took the initiative and left unconcerned parents. These youths, nonetheless, have a range of possible resolutions for any situation It is, then, their choice to remain living in the streets. It is a choice that these youths perceive as realistic. Not all youths can accommodate the haphazard placements, foster homes, or other official responses. Summarily, a regular accommodation chosen by youths is to first leave the dysfunctional home. Once they leave the home, there is a potential for several trajectories such as the voluntary status of living with relatives or friends or the choice to marry a non street person Even the involuntary status of a state placement is a choice—it is possible to run away from a placement. Another accommodation belongs in between these two and is a common fate for out-of-home youths: joining the street culture.

This property I have focused on (joining street culture as an accommodation) has many dimensions. These dimensions include the intensity of anger between youths and families, the degree of family dysfunction, the age or timing involved in when the youths leave, the duration and number of leavings, the act of leaving itself, with or without assistance, the potential for consequences, and the cycles of interface between the youth, the family, the social service, or the juvenile system.

Contexts

In axial coding, the context relates to both the phenomenon and the action/interaction strategies directed towards managing the phenomenon. The context for street youths is the conditions within which they make their accommodations. My focus is on their interior or personal conditions.

These are the tools in their bag of accommodation tricks and include their capabilities, skills, creative talents, and all other personal powers they perceive to be at their disposal. The activity of accommodating to the loss by leaving the home results in the context of youths needing to marshal their particular set of tools. These tools include both strengths and weaknesses, both positives and negatives, and these qualities are organically capable of growing or shrinking.

Other properties that are part of the context are the personal environmental attributes of the youths, such as their age, IQ, sexual orientation, level of education, degree of trauma received in the former home, and psychological disposition. My focus became the youths' development and use of tools or survival oriented attitudes needed to psychologically accommodate the loss of a functional family. My study found five tools: developing egalitarian relationships, having a recreational unit, finding an opportunity to contribute, seeking responsibility, creating a sense of agency.

Intervening Conditions

The broader and general conditions bearing on the youths' action strategies are the resources external to them. This specific set is the one available to the youths living the street lifestyle.

A prime resource for youths is the variety of services made available through various agencies. A typical list of services and resources includes: emergency needs, employment counseling, adult social work, family reconciliation, intensive therapy, outreach, housing strategies, court advocacy, drug and alcohol counseling, aftercare follow-up, and general medical care. Other factors that are part of the formal services but are less explicit have an influence on the youths. These factors include a stable casework relationship, investment in services for youth, age-appropriate staff response, availability of an off-street social network, and tolerance of youths by the service staff. Other legitimate as well as underground services available to the youths include religious and private charitable organizations, pimp-controlled prostitution, drug-selling opportunities, fencing networks for stolen goods, and the generosity of citizens towards panhandling youths.

Action/Interaction

In axial coding, action/interaction is a set of strategies designed or directed towards managing or handling the phenomenon. It is the variety of ways the youths respond to the loss under the restraints of the contexts and conditions of their environment. Several properties for this category can be listed for the youths and include such replacement actions as starting a new family, joining a foster family or rejoining the original family, or participating in a street family context.

The replacement strategy I focused on is the acknowledgment and participation in the street family context. Further, I focused on the specifics of the mythological features of the street family, including art, origins, myths to live by, heroes of the past, religion, and social classification schemes. Other dimensions of living the street family context include the following street family rules: defining your street family members, places, or squats; and, being able to relate a family history. Consequences of these actions and interactions (in my study a replacement behavior that acknowledges the street family context) are as follows: actions and interactions are taken in response to the loss, or to manage the loss have outcomes or consequences. These results are not always what was intended or predicted, and sometimes they are not even consciously connected to the behaviors.

Basically, the youths' first level outcome would be to reduce the anxiety or emptiness left by the loss. The practical, external consequences of replacing the original family with a street family can be any level of success or failure. Some youths successfully leave street life before the age range of 18-21 years. Other youths simply grow biologically and never achieve a psychological or developmental maturity.

Several limitations related to the methodology should be mentioned, although all were apparent at the outset of the study and were accepted as such. First of all, the retrospective data requested in the interviews are a limitation. Memories that have undergone possible repression and retrieval as well as cognitive and affective processing over a period of years may contribute to distortions of reporting. While such distortions constitute unintentional misrepresentation of the facts, they must be accepted. When we seek the respondent's phenomenology, though, these misrepresented facts can be problematic. All self-report is in some sense suspect, but, one hopes, deliberate misrepresentation and omission can, in fact, be avoided. Second, this study is one of perception. Healing from abusive and dysfunctional family backgrounds is an evolving process. Perceptions can be ever changing as individuals continue to grow. Finally, nothing was proved or disproved by this qualitative research, as is inherently true of all exploratory research.

IV

Getting to Know Street Youths

A TYPICAL DAY ON THE STREET

A lesson to be learned from this study is how much street youth culture is a reflection of the parent culture. While the youths live an obviously extraordinary lifestyle, the forms and functions they experience are not unknown to the parent culture. For example, one youth provided a depiction of his day. During a conversation we had in December, he started to explain a typical day:

> I begin very early by sleeping. It's cold out and the morning can't be endured unless you are asleep. I've been using a sleeping bag, just under the steps at *The Tin* [a youth agency], which opens at 9:00 a.m.
>
> When *The Tin* opens, I go inside to get warm and my blood circulating. I can get warm at the malls also; the Gala opens at 7:30. Sometimes I need things from the Tin, like a bus ticket. After scrounging for something to eat, I can go take a shower and get a change of clothes at G-house. When you use the shelter, you get a shower each night if you want. And you get a meal and you have a locker.
>
> The middle of my day is spent keeping warm. On weekends I use the Downtown Market. Other days the malls and cafes work, as long as I behave myself. Some places get after us and 86 us. I like to panhandle outside stores during

Christmas. It keeps me in money for coffee, drugs, and
clothes. There's not much else to do and nothing more
important.

My day isn't over 'til late and I can't always predict
where I'll end up each day. By late night, I've probably
crashed somewhere. You're not always safe on the steps at
the Tin. The big need is to find a safe spot.

This youth has described a range of behaviors that specifically suit his
unique resource base. He is pursuing the basic needs for human
physical survival. He's finding shelter, food, and basic personal
hygiene in an economic niche that provides a somewhat scarce
amount of goods. And yet it seems a similar set of pursuits to those
core activities of an at-home youth. The at-home youth may have
greater access to the materials of survival, but both youths are left
with leisure time to fill. It is the similarities of street youths' lives in
comparison to at-home youths that caught my attention. The ways
that the youths are similar piqued my curiosity to find the ways the
two cultures are different.

This study did not begin with the day in my life story quoted. I
had been collecting data long before his contribution. However, that
narrative might be identified as an important decision-making event. I
had not yet known where to start the narrowing of the study of this
unfamiliar culture. A number of starts had already been unsatisfactory.
Thus, my fortuitous discovery of similarities and differences between
the way that the two cultures meet basic human needs highlights the
fact that some youths live at home and the other group has no
home/family. That is obvious, but I had not yet consciously
articulated the observation. Perhaps, I decided, now I should try to
understand and examine more closely what "no home" means. This
focus was different, and it was a necessary start towards my
exploration of what street culture is.

It is Mannheim's (1966) view of group ideology that gives
ultimate direction to this study. The judgments from the street youths
become an integrated system of thought and, thus, establish the total
conception. Becker and Geer (1960) continue this line of reasoning,
giving the set of youths' responses the value of building a partial
model of their cultures. A total model can come afterwards.

Youths' Statements About Street Families

The similarity I first noted is fairly straightforward and does not yield any greater depth or advancement in the understanding of the street culture. I decided to undertake a more thorough study with a narrower focus. In my effort to produce a description that would lead to a fuller understanding of the lives of street youths, I had to start with a small finding about their lives. The search for similarities or differences between street youths and at-home youths began with what street youths often spoke of as the street family. This entity, though curiously never clearly defined, can be found in the literature about and by street youths. But, interestingly enough, the term "street family" has no listings or citings in the social science abstracts. I found the street family mentioned anecdotally in a few training manuals produced by local social service agencies. Those manuals instructed trainees to respect a street family and to avoid speaking negatively about the influence of the street family or its members.

Certainly, I had heard frequent use of the term street family, and yet I had never met one. I had grown used to meeting youths in their natural settings alone, in pairs. or in groups of familiar friends, but I had never been told, "This is my family." At this point, I developed a few interview questions to guide my conversations with the youths. While they very often gave concrete answers and definitions to my questions, they were not responding to the street family questions with the concrete answers at-home adolescents could be expected to give. I had expected something like "I have three sisters and a father, and we live in a squat under the bridge." Any variation about who and/or where would be a sign of life or of a quickening to the concept.

Each time I prompted the discussion of street families by asking a question and each time I alluded to the term in casual conversation, no one responded to or defined the term "street families." Why were the youths' responses seemingly avoiding my question, and where were the parameters? In fact, a definition of anything that is a listing of parameters is one that has named the independent variables or the constants. It would be a definition that describes the form but not the general nature of the subject. Since the constants or form of the street family were not revealed, I decided that perhaps I should try to discover its general nature or functions.

Street family descriptions emerged from the data. The descriptions were derived by using both guided interviews (Table 1) and observations of youths in dialogue, either among themselves or during spontaneous participation with me. It was typical for the youths to describe street family from their own idiosyncratic perspectives, and, therefore, they seemingly described a capricious, almost fantastic, entity:

- My family is not here.
- I t comes and goes, and today it's gone.
- [Three names] . . . [pause] . . . a very interesting group of people.
- We have to move a lot, so we're broken up now.
- I can't tell you names; we are sworn to secrecy.
- Let's see, that's a good question that I can't answer.
- It's everybody and nobody.
- Those who will help you no matter what, or those who don't kill you no matter what.
- The ones I love are Bradley and Kristy.
- The people in your squat.
- I don't leave anyone out; it's not smart to cut out someone who might love you.
- It's overrated.
- Everyone you have sex with or will have sex with.

Street Family Interview Guide Questions:

- Tell me about the street family. Who's in it?
- How do street families help each other?
- What does your street family do for you?
- How do street families differ from street friendships?
- What will happen to your street family in the future?
- What are your beliefs about street families?
- Tell me about belonging.
- If your family needs help, how far will you go?
- Who can you depend on?

Youths' Statements About Ideal Families

Such a variety of responses! The youths' quotations about street family do not represent a calculated frequency or distribution of all youths' responses. Instead, the significance of the street family or any phenomenon in a naturalistic study is looked at for the social effects. The idiosyncratic responses are a clue that I need to look at them from the perspective of a patternmaker—someone who can see the forest because of the trees. This stage of inductive reasoning leads me back into the forest to gather more data on the trees. Ideally, I am going to code and categorize these basic units of data into some sort of organized category. My search for the social effects of the street family (no longer a fact-in-evidence concept) begins with looking for functional equivalents. Do street youth accommodate and perhaps replace the lost real and/or idealized family function. I continued to rely on basic axial coding processes to build models toward a larger paradigm for the street youth culture. Therefore, I graduated the study to one of the provisional categories to direct me out of my unsuccessful search observable reality of street family.

I examined the provisional category of the youths' conception of the perfect family. Representations of the ideal included the following:

- The way others are; good and bad.
- It's just a label.
- They're very scary people.
- Leave me out of that one. How would I know?
- A source of truth and caring.

It is not a surprise that street youths do not answer questions with what social scientists consider operationalized definitions. The bottom line is, I still have vague answers to two questions so far in my investigation: "What are the street families?" and "What are the perfect families?" I noticed I had devised a continuum for future typologies and put these two constructs on opposite ends. These two constructs, which are apparent pillars of each respective culture, are eluding my attempts to find them in the youths' words.

Understandably, the social and political scientists still struggle to fix the boundaries of the normative or statistically average family. Therefore, a standard for a tight comparison does not even exist.

Case History Summaries

This was the time to apply the technique of flip-flop. Hoping to enhance my theoretical sensitivity, I began making comparisons at the extremes of the dimensions. Temporarily I considered both the street family and the ideal family to not yet be visible, and I examined the youths' recollection of their lives with their families of origin. I selected the stories of youths who provided me with sufficient information to tell a family history. I chose these particular youths because their stories reflected a range of family experiences and yet were typical enough to not distort the sense of street youths as a group. Some details of the stories have been disguised to maintain confidentiality.

Andy

Andy is a 16-year-old who considers himself a Native-American. When Andy was five, school counselors told his parents that he had a "mental disease." Andy used to destroy things and harm other children at school. He feels today that his problems were why his father left the family. Andy hated school and was never successful.

Andy's mother tried to get professional help for him, but his problems persisted, so his mother sent Andy to live with his father. Andy's stepmother resented the trouble he caused and eventually would not let him stay in her home. Andy remembers stealing money from her when she was intoxicated and sleeping. Andy was 10 when he was returned to his mother. She had remarried and his stepfather was an alcoholic. Andy avoided going home for as long as he could each night and often slept during the day after being on his own all night. He was expelled from school "too many times to remember."

Even though the family lived in a rural area, Andy was able to find a small set of homosexual boys in the area. His activities with the gay lifestyle grew, and today Andy identifies himself as a gay youth. He never told his parents, in part because they were members of a church that preaches that homosexuality is a sin.

Andy ran away from home at the age of 14 and has never recontacted his family. His early street life was very violent, and Andy was involved with juvenile authorities "all the time." He has prostituted most of his time on the street and was recently tested for HIV antibodies. He said the test was positive. Currently, Andy knows about safe sex techniques and still prostitutes to survive. He uses very few of the social services such as counseling and training. The services he appreciates and sometimes uses include those that provide food or clothing when he's cold, hungry, and broke.

Rose

Rose is a 17-year-old redhead. At the time of my field contacts, she was living in a youth shelter. She had one month of eligibility remaining, and it was wintertime.

Rose's time with her family of origin was marked by neglect, disorganization, and instability. Her biological father did not live with her biological mother, and he rarely came for visits. Rose thinks it was during summertime when he would visit for about a day or two or a full weekend. She lived with her mother for the first 15 years, except for one summer when she was living with a relative. Rose did not remember who he was in the family network. Rose thinks she was 11 years old at the time. Her mother had been hospitalized for a medical problem and Rose and her younger sister did not like being at an unfamiliar relative's house.

There were no men in her mother's household, and Rose never developed a relationship with the male relative she lived with for the one summer. Thus, a fatherfigure has been absent from her household environment throughout her childhood and early adolescence development.

At age 11, Rose had a sexual experience with a neighbor boy. He molested her in her backyard and tried to repeat the incident several times again over the following week. Rose believes he sodomized her and feels she let it happen. She didn't tell anyone about the molestation.

At age 15, Rose ran away from her mother's house. Rose felt, "Mom was so boring and kind of dull. I had to get out of there." Rose felt that her younger sister could take care of the mother, because, in Rose's words, her mother,

> didn't do anything around the house but yell for us to fetch this, do that, and be quiet. We never had clean clothes or food fixed. I was ashamed when people came to our place. It was always a mess.

Over the next two years, Rose was placed in a foster care home two times. Yet, those homes lasted only a short month or few weeks before Rose had problems with the foster parents, other youths in the home, or the rules that she "didn't think were meant for girls like me." She felt she was adult enough to not need rules and needed help only with a room and money. Rose feels that the youths in foster care placements were "sheep and children." Rose did run away occasionally for a night on the street where things were "fast, hot, and real." By the time she had run away from the two foster homes a few times, she was "ready for full-time independence. I've used up all they have to offer. They didn't help me or get me what I craved."

Rose now had street contacts and knew a little bit about street life and its networks. She felt she was old enough to take care of herself. She calculated she'd been on the streets for about a year and a half when I met her. Rose says she prostituted only a few times with some friends who taught her the basics. Rose began to use the agencies and youth services right away and continues to hang out with other youths who are familiar and adept at using social services.

John

John was 16 when I first met him in the park. John has a street family that allows him to sleep in the various apartments that friends are letting them use. John does not always go with them and has an outside set of friends who also share resources with him. Occasionally, he is out on the street all night at 24-hour cafes, or in the park, in an unlocked car, or the like.

John's early life, to age 10, was generally stable, and he enjoyed living in a two-parent secure home. Then his mother got sick, lingered, and died, and his father increased his drinking to the rate that he "was always doing it." Soon, John's father, whether drunk or sober, began to physically abuse John. John moved in with his father's brother for a year, and that was satisfactory for all until that uncle was diagnosed with AIDS.

Then John moved back with his father, and at age 13 John began to experiment with drugs that his school mates provided. John had been bright and cooperative at school, but things quickly went downhill. His father responded angrily and with physical violence when the school counselors would set up parent-teacher meetings. Trouble at home escalated and one night John was kicked out. His father did not file a missing child report when John never came back. John left the southern state small town and hitchhiked up to the largest metropolitan area in Oregon, one with the largest network of displaced youths.

John quickly found the drug and music culture in town to be very attractive and became fully committed to that lifestyle. He tried every drug available and began to deal (sell) drugs to keep up his lifestyle and to support his addiction to drugs. He says that today that habit is in the past and that it's too rough to keep that pace of life up for long. John's been through several street-based programs for addicts. Yet he still uses drugs and alcohol occasionally to regularly and it is a constant goal to quit altogether.

In retrospect, John talks about how his father showed him how to avoid life's hard times by using the escape of drugs. He thinks he should have gone into the opposite behavior to get away from the trouble that his father was in; it felt like such a bad example. Yet John feels he is now living just like his father, and John's one solace is that he did not have any kids to beat up and disappoint.

John does not recall any childhood sexual experiences that were traumatic and considers himself to have a "normal heterosexual" orientation. He has never prostituted, but was beaten up once on the streets for being in the company of gay prostituting friends. He thought the men who beat him up were from a group that has a reputation for gay bashing. John claims he will do anything to avoid getting into a fight.

Finding the Historical Origins of the Youths

Some of my earliest sit-down interviews were with youths who were happy to tell the story of their lives. They knew, I was writing a book about them and were delighted at the opportunity to "tell the world what it's been like to be me."

These three case history summaries are from information the youths provided to me in purposeful discussions. The actual content of their oral histories was far more elaborate and colorful than my summaries. Indeed, my first opportunity to take a history from a youth left me overwhelmed, confused and panicked. Historical benchmarks were few, and I defensively concluded I did not need to know the year of their first set of parents divorce. I clearly was not likely to get those data anyway. Overall, I heard seemingly very chaotic streams of consciousness.

My concern was how to sort the fantastic variety of information in the youth's life stories. I suspected that two levels of reporting were happening as I sat listening to the youths talk. They were (a) recounting in their best efforts a presentation of historical events, while (b) trying to relate and reveal some of the subtexts of their unresolved history of traumatic childhoods. I was not writing notes while they were talking, and, after ten minutes I began to be grateful. Originally, I was going to note and remember outlines, to be verified and filled in during a second interview. Soon I developed a plotline theme for the general storytelling behaviors I saw in the early and subsequent interviews. A standard plotline theme included the following three types of plots: a few pieces of remembered personal events in any sequence; a few pieces of rumored family stories; and a few pieces of imported history, often borrowed or integrated from friends, the media, or fantasy. I assumed all three plotlines were accurate and distorted at the same time.

Facts did exist and the youths sometimes could tell me the years of their sets of parents' divorces. I decided not to attempt to verify or triangulate the dates or actuality of such events; not that I could have anyway. My dilemma was what to do about the numerous abortions, or pregnancies and childbirths, or rock and roll bands formed, or careers as a writer, or murders they had witnessed, or countries they had lived in, or big cars they had owned. What was I to do with their imported histories? All of these accomplishments were part of the histories of the 14, 15, 16, 17, 18-year-old youths I was meeting. I chose to include this history telling behavior and the degree to which these street youths practice it to form the following story line.

Within axial coding, the causal condition is the painful, disturbing, and often repressed or blanked-out actual history of a child. The phenomenon or event that follows is the child's need to avoid, erase, or change a painful past. The context is simply the fact that nothing will change that past. Intervening conditions are the opportunities that youths find or are given to remember and tell their history. Now the action youths can practice is to import or create a new history and to be socially or personally witnessed as the owner of a new, improved early life. The consequences are a variety of relief and an improved self-concept the youth can enjoy, regardless of whether anyone else believes the history.

The above story line is my interpretation of a phenomenon that becomes one of the unique and culturally germane perspectives of the study's informants. I hope that I have properly located the youths' behavior, its interpretation, and its accurate placement within their culture. I hope that this product of analysis is one of the many findings that help make my model comprehensible. It is, after all, a prototype for other and larger coding schemes. That is, the concept of youths taking the action/interaction (a stage in axial coding) strategies in efforts to change their lives has become central to my study.

V

Functions of Street Families

THE TASK-PERFORMING FUNCTIONS OF TOOLS

A variety of frameworks (i.e., exchange and choice, conflict theory, symbolic interaction, family stress theory) have been applied to the family phenomenon, and they all aid in some understanding of families. A systems framework is very comprehensive and offers abstract concepts under four primary headings of (a) task performance and functions, (b) interdependence and interaction between and among component parts and relational networks, (c) boundary maintenance, and (d) equilibrium and adaptation, and all within the frame of their environment (Hill, 1971).

Zimmerman (1987) claims the task-performing property of social systems pertains to the functions they are expected to perform. The primary functions families as social systems are expected to perform include (a) physical maintenance and care of family members; (b) addition of new members through procreation or adaption and their relinquishment when they mature; (c) socialization of children for adult roles, such as those of spouse parent, worker, neighbor, voter, and community member; (d) social control of members, which refers to the maintenance of order within the family and groups external to it; (e) production and consumption of goods and services needed to support and maintain the family unit; and (f) maintenance of family morale and motivation to ensure task performance both within the family and in other social groups. How families perform these tasks varies with such factors as ethnic and religious background, socioeconomic status, particulars of family members, the urgency of the tasks themselves, family life cycle stage, and the location in which they live.

The task-performing functions of the family are some of the more concrete within the family as viewed through the framework of the social systems theorists. When street life, in particular street family life, is considered within this framework, it suggests yet another answer to the question of why it is so easy for youth to become assimilated into street culture. The creation of a street family context that understands, accepts, and accommodates the conceptual framework that youths have in the streets can help solidify and stabilize membership in the culture.

My study shows that a number of provisions and task-performing functions that help solidify a normative (parent culture) family can be found in the street family context. My five germinal categories or functions reflect groupings that came out of my data. They are organized under the axial code key of context and as a group are labeled tools. I use the word tools to capture the range of skills, talents, interpretations, perceptual abilities, psychological flexibility, developmental attainment, etc., that are necessary for street youths to achieve the accommodation of the loss. In fact, these tools are merely one property under the context code.

All the properties under context represent a variety of traits the youths bring to the streets. Some examples of traits that are not directly translated as tools include age, gender, intelligence, physical strength or health, past academic success or failure, degree of trauma at home, religious background, and racial or other diversity prejudices and experiences. All these traits are important and relevant, yet as Strauss and Corbin (1990) point out, I must first formulate and commit other categories.

But then, the methodological task of this study is to find and follow a fictive pathway through this culture. I am not looking for one index youth who would provide valid and reliable data to represent the whole culture. I am tracing a possible pathway and observing the variety of youth views as each one of my informants provides a unique reality.

Five primary task-performing properties are evident within the data: (a) seeking responsibility, (b) developing egalitarian relationships, (c) having a recreational unit, (d) finding the opportunity to contribute, and (e) creating a sense of agency. When I use the gerund, I have transformed the verb into a noun and can then describe the youths' activities as tools to be used in accommodating the loss.

Seeking Responsibility

Attaining a sense of appropriate responsibility is especially difficult when youths have come from a dysfunctional family of origin:

> My mom used to holler at me all the time. Like if she ran out of money at the end of the month. I guess I was supposed to do something because I cost so much. Shit, she was always losing money on her nights out . . . looking for a new boyfriend. We kids started to eat next door. Then I didn't eat at her house at all. I didn't need her money for nothing.

In this instance, the youth's sense of responsibility and reciprocal rights is based on a distorted family norm. Though she felt she had friends on the street, she was not interested in "being in a street-family." She continues:

> I used to prostitute while I was at the shelter. They never knew I was lying. They're all too busy or easy. They are, but can't stop me from doing what I need and they won't give me. Even if they know, I'll still want to work camp [prostitute].

The street youths are often more confused than at-home youths during the transition between leaving a dependable source of basic needs and gaining responsibility for their own basic needs.

> I left town last month because there was this concert in [out-of-state-city] that I could go to. I was going out of town for the first time in a while. I was afraid to go because I'd miss my [drug and alcohol] group, but music means a lot to me. I live for it. Of course, I drank and used up there. I was happy up there. But I'm home now. I go to group. When I got back home, even though it's the streets, I saw that Jan had been using while I was gone. That was my sad fuck-up.

Even while the youths have an exaggerated and inappropriate sense of responsibility, the street-family network provides a framework within which to learn and practice the dynamics of responsibility. Youths do have to accept responsibility to continue functioning in their networks of street friends and families. The following statements reflect their views of responsibility.

> • I can't go back to [a circle of friends] because I stole
>   their dope.
> • After I stopped baby-sitting her kid, I had to move on.
> • I lost my job and by then they were gone; I mean they
>   had new people I didn't know.

Developing Egalitarian Relationships

Youth often feel ill at ease in social situations. For displaced youths, their chances to be satisfactorily socialized have been limited. Assimilation into street culture eases some of the tensions they experienced earlier. Their family of origin's atmosphere usually was not an opportunity to receive fair or egalitarian treatment.

Other Adults and Nonegalitarian Treatment

Even the street-connected adult contacts that are available to displaced youths can continue the pattern of disrespect and of failure to understand or fulfill the deep hunger for self-esteem. Agencies offer services and attitudes that youths view negatively:

> • They treat you like dirt; they don't do nothing for you. They
>   don't care.
> • I was wary—it [help] was hard to take.
> • They treated me like it was charity.
> • I decided I didn't need the services.
> • They asked me to change.

- I was supposed to attend meetings where they say what's wrong with me.
- I felt like a lowly bum there.

Often youths feel betrayed in agency situations where organizational goals and contexts of youth specific services are not more strongly based on human relations models. This youth population is especially sensitive and intimidated by service delivery models that cannot be flexible in balancing bureaucratic demands with youths injured emotional needs. It is sometimes stated that the government cannot parent these youths, and that policy does leave displaced youths searching. Other adult to youth relationships are more patently exploitive. These adults include pimps, johns (men who buy prostitutes), sugar daddies, dope sellers. fences, and the like.

- I've been beat up by lots of tricks [johns].
- We all get raped in the city.
- Pimps control the money I earn.
- [Drug supplier] just gives me a hit [sample of the drug] and then I'm too loaded to take care of myself.

Belonging in Your Own Turf

Street youths own almost nothing. Whatever material they possess for the moment is likely to be stolen or given away or left behind for lack of storage space. Often the youths will own only the clothes on their backs. Youths in a family can feel like certain geographical hangouts, turfs, cafes or cafe booths, park sections, or the like belong to them. It is a small claim to ownership and status in a property-oriented world.

- We guys and girls get tired of sleeping under trees and in shelters. Just the thing we need is housing. The first step for my buddies is to have a case manager get us a big palatial place to stay. Now, our best spot is [under a bridge overpass], but another group of gang bangers are hassling us. We'll

need to move all of us, try to stick together. We
need to hold our ground.
• Our favorite is in [a poetry cafe] and where we have
meetings others can't hang out with us.
• I know how to locate [a friend] because her sisters
and brothers like to do video games. It's their turf,
the video freaks.
• I won't go to a street lined with gay-oriented
business because I'm not gay or bisexual or like
them at all.

It is important for the members of this rejected population to find a
setting where nonjudgmental tolerance and acceptance occur. Larger
society and many segments of street cultures have not been able to
overlook physical differences and cultural diversities among
themselves. Bigotry and discrimination are embraced by some street
families and can be shielded by particular families.

• I know that suicide is a girl's way out.
• Anyone goes to a pimp must be a tard.
• Faggots are AIDS bait.
• Breeders always get the housing if they are pregnant.
• He is from a skin-head group that needs to be locked
up.
• There is way too much violence in [the section of
town where adult homeless gather]. Those people
don't love each other.

Youths who identify with a family network have appreciably been
granted membership in spite of their acknowledged idiosyncrasies or
differences.

• We let all that gossip about drugs and AIDS bother
other people. Like we could get gang-banged any
day. Prejudice equals ignorance and we know the
score on safe sex. John is a respected member of our
family and a very beautiful queen.

- God saved us when he sent to us this littlest daughter. She's lucky she found us because we love her very much. There is nothing for her to fear. [She has a limp.]

A Place to Feel Normal

An opportunity to feel normal can be provided by an accepting family of street peers. It is a place to conform to a different standard.

- Street life isn't normal, you know; we can evaporate any day out here.

- It's not clean where I live, not like regular folks.

- To be normal for me would be to stop, get a job at Fred Meyer's, and stop selling myself.

- What do I have a life for? I have a conviction that no one loves me. The justification for committing suicide is a dilemma.

Typical street youths are without jobs or have unstable access to a job. They lack shelter and have no reliable and honest source of other basic needs. Nonetheless, they have available some transitioning or remedial programs that are uniquely designed to help them exit the street culture and lifestyle.

- I'm Fred and I am 17 years old and have been living on the street and the shelter for the last few years. I'm engaged to be married to a very wonderful, special person.

- I'm attempting to get my shit together, my life in order, and get off the streets. But some people are not very eager for me to acquire my freedom. Bidi cries when I talk like I want to leave.

Having a Recreational Unit

Street youths have an abundance of free time. They are similar to others of their age in that adolescence is a stage of accelerated physical growth and an abounding amount of energy. The struggle for survival, foraging for the basic needs of food, shelter, clothing, is an activity that non-street youths do not engage in. In-home youth have families that provide the basic services for survival. Typically, families also provide the basic function and form for a recreational and leisure environment.

The unique set of circumstances for street youths develops because they must do work to survive: find and conform to food line or soup kitchen protocol, avoid violation of agency rules in order to maintain access to clothes and personal hygiene items, show up on time, and otherwise conform to the regulations of formal shelters and/or informal street spaces. Other work includes learning the ropes and limits to engaging in such illegal, yet financially gainful, activities as prostitution, drug entrepreneurship, and stealing for profit. It is this full set of otherwise adult behaviors that street youths engage in that needs to be balanced or neutralized by recreation. This leisure can normalize their life best if it is engaged in with other youths. It is difficult to find and constructively fill recreational time amongst youths with few material resources.

- It's usually not worth the trouble to learn sports; they just make me feel worse.

- I love the concerts at the [park], but I hate the yuppies on roller blades. They're snotty and rude.

- Walking around all night is not my idea of aerobic exercise; it just means I've got nowhere to go.

- Hanging out in [the town square] is easier if you're not by yourself.

- The art museum has free admission on certain days of the month.

- [An agency for youths] used to have a sports program thing organized.

- Sometimes when I've scored [gotten money], I
  really like to treat my family to a good movie.

- Last summer I organized a hitch-hike vacation for us
  [four friends] to my home state. It started off great,
  but John didn't make it back here and that was a
  bummer.

- It's safer to do certain things with a close group of
  street friends; you can make your statement.

- I like the shelter staff because they taught me pool.
  But they have age rules there and can kick you out.
  I like to play pool there for free and want to teach
  what I know to the kids.

Street youth are not resource-poor; they discover and enjoy activities
together.

Finding Opportunities to Contribute

Street youths have too few opportunities to contribute. The ability to
give something helps move the critical power imbalance in their
favor. Giving their possessions to others is a common behavior and
the roots of this behavior are complex, including maintaining
appropriate participation in the street economy. However, the family
context in the streets is an opportunity for participation in a social
and psychological exchange network.

The developmental delays experienced by many of these youths
during their injurious childhoods often result in a passive victim
psychology. This psychology is based on the perception of events—
both good and bad as external to the self and random. Developmental
approaches to growth emphasize building self-confidence, including
feelings of contribution.

A Place to Teach

A component of family is the concept of age gradients and the rewarding task of more experienced members sharing their wisdom with younger or less experienced members. When the teaching is regarding moral lessons, youths practice retroflexive reformation or internalizing information by teaching it to others.

- I used to be slaved by my pimp, but now I'm trying to be like Shari who tells me pimps are as low as rapists, molesters, and murderers.

- I learned everything about my pregnancy from Janis who had her baby last year.

- I didn't understand RAP music until I joined Ed and them all.

- It's good when I can steer our kids to the righteous way.

- Now that I'm the oldest, I'm the dad and I bore them with all my lectures—just kidding.

- When I write about myself, it seems wasteful, so I like to write poetry about someone else and show them how I feel about them.

The youths express negative feelings when they are frustrated in their attempts to contribute.

- It makes me feel creepy when they don't like my ideas.

- It's like it's charity, too pitiful to only get donations.

- I get taxed [street for robbed] when they give me free stuff that I don't ask for.

Role Modeling

Role modeling within a family context is a favorable time for youths to build self-esteem. It is isolating when they lack the opportunity to be authentic, to be witnessed in their authenticity and thereby be affirmed for being who they are.

- On the street you need to be tough; strangers will not respect you if you're not.

- You can't take a chance when you're alone; don't let anyone catch you.

- When I'm getting in someone's car [to prostitute], you can't be yourself. You're thinking and acting like an empty soul to be used like a doll.

- It's truly hard to disappoint the counselors; you just smile and whatever.

- Question: Who is the child of which I speak? Why do we hide the most likable and precious part of ourselves?

Youths can reduce this psychological isolation and bolster self-esteem when they work together and identify with peers.

- My goal is to offer life-saving information in a creative and entertaining way [when acting in the "Gorilla Theater"]. Nothing compares to the happiness I get by influencing people to change their dangerous habits. Saving lives. And that, my friends, is what life is all about.

- Life on the street is a bowl full of rotten cherries, and it's my job to keep the bowl full. I don't have a job yet, but I'm in the job readiness program and I'm trying to get Carolyn to come with me.

- I wanted to be with people who could afford Doc Martens [a type of shoe].

- I've made a tee-shirt that I wear for my friends. It shows how to put a condom on a dildo. Great, huh?

- Quizzes and tests aren't as hard as living on the streets. I'm working on my GED because Pat showed me how to sign up when he did.

- When we go to the X-ray [youth club], I help by hustling the best spot and free food.

- I joined with them because they were anti-racists skin heads.

Creating Personal Agency

Youths benefit from being involved in the variety of internal housekeeping functions of their family networks. Within that context, those functions include decision-making, organizing internal and external protocols, maintaining family or group boundaries, operating family discipline styles, and developing and practicing cooperative communication and relationship skills. It helps them learn to make self-controlled decisions.

Children in mainstream families develop their sense of self within the family's structure and relatedness roles (Zimmerman, 1988). A street family also provides an opportunity for filling family positions. The youths can practice their performances and experience the burden and rewards of fulfilling the duties of decision-making tasks.

The family context in the streets is similar to the general family in which decisions are made formally and informally.

- We watch out for each other. It's our sacred duty.

- If you don't like the music we play, bring something better.

- When you don't go with them, you feel left out.

- After we all talked about Robin, we had a vote at
the end.

- Tim wouldn't stop preaching about sin, so we
decided to play an April Fools joke on him.

Organizing Internal and External Protocols

The group's rules in a family system revolve around interaction and
reciprocal positions. Thus, the safety and maintenance of the family
depend upon the understanding and successful performance of the rules
and norms (Zimmerman, 1988). A personal sense of agency is
difficult to establish without a social context in which the youths can
articulate their rule-making behaviors. This function helps the youths
solidify a base from which they can more safely operate in their
particular street environment.

- No is something you scream in an emergency.

- Survival first, don't mess with that one.

- Kids, parents, and family care about you. Call them
up on occasion.

- Don't rat [reveal family business].

- Always know where you are and where you can find
us .

- Don't bring your loser friends here.

- Everyone is different.

- Don't be using heroin in front of us.

- Don't touch my honey.

- Carefully wander the streets.

- Jail is not a great place; don't commit crimes that
  will take you there.

Maintaining Family or Group Boundaries

Katz and Kahn (1966) describe family boundary patterns as
interactions that differ in degree and kind from those that occur
between families and the external organizations and people in their
environment. Street youths as a group are largely abandoned by or
invisible to mainstream interventionists. However, the youths more
often feel threatened by peer groups, street gangs, or other similar
entities. Once the boundaries are learned, the constant support for
them is a unifying exercise.

- Victims, you know who you are, aren't allowed
  here.

- You make the first move and we'll clean up the
  streets with your sorry ass.

- We all carry this kind of knife [under four inches and
  legal].

Operating Family Discipline Styles

The notion of equilibrium assumes a range of possible states within
which a family as a system presumably can function and to which it
can adapt (Hill, 1971). Street families will also develop patterns of
discipline and interaction in conformity with the range of norms
members share. The youths are vigilant and often display a law and
order orientation.

• If you break a rule, you leave town.

• We never voted or nothing, but we just sort of knew we had to punish her.

• After our stuff was thrown out of the apartment, John got asked to find his own home.

Development and Practice of Cooperative Communication and Relationship Skills

The state of equilibrium of a social system is made possible through negative and positive feedback (Hill 1971). Thus families seek out and use information about outside systems to facilitate and maintain self awareness (Zimmerman, 1988). Street family members view feedback as instructive and system enhancing. Youths develop and practice relationship skills primarily in social contexts such as the street family.

• Other people are affected by you.

• People can help; ask them.

• Good things happen to those who you listen to.

• When you stop feeling welcome, you know you did something wrong and you're on the road again.

• Don't bother to beg for pity, just beg for freedom.

VI

Ritual and Mythological Features of Street Families

REPLACEMENT BEHAVIORS

The axial coding category depicting which action/interaction strategies are chosen by the youths is named *replacement behaviors*. Following my story line, these youths have decided to leave behind the original family, the formal replacements available, or both. The behavior/phenomenon being studied after this antecedent loss of family is the youths' accommodations to the loss. The youths this study focuses on are the ones whose chosen pathway is to engage in replacement behaviors. There are a range and a variety of such behaviors used by each youth. Three major choices are (a) start a new biological or real family through the regular empirical pathways (i.e., a parent unit makes a baby); (b) join a foster family or reconcile and rejoin the original family; and (c) participate in the street family context, or reify the assorted street features that are family like. Up to this point, the use of *tools* has served to succeed the loss of family functions, features, services, and opportunities for growth. There is, however, more work to be done by the youths who are striving to replace that larger, holistic context of family.

Axial coding is a transactional system possessing certain properties. These properties include interactive and interrelated levels of conditions, action/interaction as the central system, action/interaction that takes place in related sequences and is processual, temporality that is built into the conditions, and, contingencies that can change conditions that facilitate or hinder action/interaction (Strauss & Corbin, 1990).

Theoretical saturation, therefore, is clearly impossible for all the properties of *replacement behaviors.* It is, in fact, beyond the scope of this research. It is not possible to capture the evolving nature of all possible events and steps leading to and located between *tool use* and *replacement* of the family. The nature of the street youths' irregular and transitory lifestyles prevented me from finding key informants whose pathways I could trace and whose changing conditions I could monitor and tally.

Ultimately, youths who have mastery over enough tools can begin *replacing behaviors and activities;* they can form a street family. They will move through the contingencies and changing conditions of the transactional system I have been outlining and reporting. One property under the replacement category leads to the formation of the street family context—or more precisely to the reification of the assortment of functions that have been replaced in some new manner.

This street family context as a property can and does, in turn, have dimensions. One dimension I found and examined is ritual and mythological features of the street family context. That dimension is what I present in the following pages. This dimension, the mythological features, is included because the mythology of any culture points out a way to perceive that group. It is a reflection and sensitive mirror of what is going on that is not always directly visible.

Myth as a System to Bring Order to Chaos

Carl Jung (1970) considers myths to be the plot, the connecting thread or the story of our life. *Myth is* derived from the Greek world *Mythas,* which means plot, action, motive, narrative; a myth is a story. Joseph Campbell (1988) reminds us that mythology is not history. James Hillman (1975) alerts us that "myths do not tell us how, they simply give us the invisible background that starts us imagining, questioning, going deeper." Christine Downing (1987) explains that discovery of the mythical patterns enhances the self-understanding. She continues to explain that an appreciation of the ways in which all the variations, transformations, and elements that go to make up the myths and patterns are integrated and necessary parts of it, is the key to the psychological understandings that emerge.

Historically speaking, human organizations, including street families or clans, develop and transmit mythological narratives about themselves, other groups, and even about fabled groups. This study highlights six aspects of mythology and the relationship of each to street youths.

Art

Lévi-Strauss determines that a myth is not something that is untrue but a shared cultural context for communication. As such, myths are ways of teaching unobservable realties by way of observable symbols (Hampden-Tumer, 1981). The contradictory nature of social life is conveyed by the bearers of tradition to novices, so that they comprehend the frustrations of the ideal by the real. Since myths are orally and visually or pictorially transmitted, there will be gaps and distortions, but a reiterated "musical score" (Hampden-Turner, 1981) conveys the structure despite missing parts. Art is a universal endeavor and a language used to represent and articulate the street experiences.

> • People who use us street kids have never read the
> poetry we write about how close we are. We share
> stories about who does what to us.

> • The Park [a church-sponsored youth dance club]
> plays techno, house and trance and serves smart
> drinks. I've heard people say it's safe there, but the
> art is so dead. I like the C [an all-ages dance club].
> You need to get high [on drugs] to really enjoy
> music.

> • I play music for my friends; it adds warmth to a
> cold existence.

- I shouldn't have narced off [told on]; everyone is
  entitled to their own opinion, but they put the
  graffiti over my wall art. It was dedicated to Pam.

- People who do street art should be paid for their
  work. It gives a message to the world.
- I use art in a personal way to express how much
  my friends mean to me.

- We did writings and religious symbols on the
  bridge to keep enemies away.

The theme running through the youths' statements about art concern
the opposites or contradictions in their lives. There is the
overvaluation of literal art or conventional art forms, which says, "We
youths are sophisticated like others in our appreciation of music,
graphic arts, literature, and dance." It is also a claim to freedom of
expression, glory, high esteem, and cultural values. On the other
hand, there is an undervaluation that is contextually embedded in how
small, vulnerable, restricted. cold. and alienated their existence is.

Origins

Myths about origins can reflect the idea that the family is a
possession, a creation of the contemporary group or members who are
tangible.

- We were meant to help each other and just bound
  ourselves in this predicament together. But it
  works
  out better than before.

- We're probably one of the smartest groups to form
  around anarchy. That's how we know we'll outlast
  the odds. We didn't feel society had a function or
  laws.

- I once belonged with a group that was like a cult. They made up their own weird religion.

- I can't hang around people who don't come from a long line of civil rights. I basically want to be with people who have their own authority. I'm a bisexual, and I've had to create my friends and family out of nowhere. We're the last group to join the struggle. It doesn't take much intelligence to be for civil rights.

A pattern to the preceding stories reveals that the ancient traditions, which often are a part of a culture's mythology, are here recent or contemporary traditions. Each youth experiences a circumscribed and young and often solitary legend. The youths then have a sense that they are the creators of their lifestyle, that there is not a classical divinity from the ethereal beyond who has created their world. As solidly and faithfully as other cultures trust their roots and their sense of belonging, street youths feel uprooted and must search for an anchor or grounding function in their own creation. Street family context serves as this touch point and, without such a context, the youths would feel psychologically abandoned and orphaned.

Myths to Live By

Stories that inform and guide street youths are often part of the lore of a clan or group that frequently hangs out together. When the family of origin and the archetypal family lessons are ill fitted to street life realities, variations seem to be devised. These equivalent myths can be warnings and can have prescriptive value.

- Street gangs that don't believe in law and order are all for the revolution. Skin heads shave their heads so they'll know who is supposed to live after the killings.

- If you are a weekend warrior [not a full-time street youth], be real, please stay at home. There are not enough for all and some gangs can have a day of sport out of you. Please stay out of our street.

- Police will arrest you right on the spot if you show that you run with the gays. They use gloves and wear face masks. I saw one cop beat up a faggot who was trying to catch up with some friends at the [gay bar].

- When winter starts to come back, you had better be tight with your family and get your squat [alternative home such as abandoned house or bridge] staked out. I heard of five friends who froze. Remember a shelter is not a permanent place to live.

- Don't let a pimp into your family; you'll all end up with him selling you.

What myths have to say about power to control is traditionally present in forms of universal order (Campbell. 1990), which is wielded by deities of ranked order.

It is my observation that street youths have a range of sources of power and control over their lives (pimps, police, weather, outsiders like weekend warriors and skin head gangs). The accommodation to the loss of a deity of ranked order (which is often symbolized as the parent figures) is for the youths to join a street family, and, in that loosely organized context, they share and assume the future responsibility for themselves and their peers. Street family titles and roles are very fluid (a mom one day is the daughter the next) and the responsibility for each member, therefore, at least feels shared. In actuality, the surrogate mother and father figure in the street family can rarely become a provider or a nurturer for each other. The youths' best efforts to gain a figment or small measure of control and power are reflected in the myths/stories of who and what to watch out for, and how to survive those threats.

Heroes from the Past

Legendary group leaders or community models are sometimes depicted as someone who could save the youths.

- Drugs, bad parents, and exploitation will bring some people to our midst who are too good to get stuck. If they're lucky enough to have a choice. I hope to find one on his way up.

- The girls who are moms have a lot to thank early moms for. Parenting classes are now here for us because a girl died in front of [a youth service agency] once and she was pregnant.

- Î used to hear about a sugar daddy [men who house youths in exchange for sexual favors] who had so much money he kept a ranch of boys in Idaho.

- A hero is someone who feeds his family.

Campbell (1990) talks about the need to transcend the earthly dangers that come from under the ground as demons or from the air as disease or that are just plain omnipresent tyrannical forces. Solutions to the everyday less demonic forces were more evident in the street youths' stories than salvation from a vague evil force. It was clear that the youths employed magical thinking in devising their heroes, and yet the heroes were often located in the here and now settings and in family contexts. Street youths' lives are often organized as a series of very concrete solutions to life-threatening and pressing problems.

Religious Beliefs

Youths turn to faith systems in both hard times and good times.

- Living with AIDS is not carefree. You think, not me, no way. But family faith will grow strong as you grow to know your illness.

- Our family worships at the altar of Poison [a
  heavy metal band] and feel like [band lead singer]
  is a god.

- We're not just bums with shopping carts; we have
  a higher spirituality than suits [people in business
  suits].

- I hate two-faced people. Could you tell me why
  Christians don't love me while I'm out here with
  my friends? Why can't I at least sleep in their God-
  damned church. I have a purer faith in people than that.

- It's not true that we worship sex, but it means we
  have too much love for them to handle.

- We burn incense to ward off evil.

While religion often represents immutability and deathlessness, or the
ever renewing of life (Downing, 1987), the earthly journeys,
representing the phases of life, are important issues in the lives of
street youths. Life and death is a linear contest in the streets. When
life and death are so prosaic, the normal range of celestial
consciousness is rarely indulged. There are few mountain tops or
Olympian playgrounds to be found. I heard youths' stories of a secular
faith vested in a church as a sleeping site, of altars for idolizing rock
stars, of sex elevated into love, and of the frequent competition to be
the best, most spiritual, or purest. The psychological underpinnings
reflect youths whose long-term vision has been shortened and
refocused on the day-to-day struggle to meet basic needs.

Fighting evil is less like the usual long-term process engaged in
by some home-bound people, and, for the youths, it is more a one on
one combat with incarnations that must be defeated by actual weapons
(incense was the weapon of choice for one youth).

- One ritual we use is the time a kid first celebrates
  a birthday on the street.

- The courage to try to sell blood is an event that's scary for our gay brothers.

- You get to be an oldtimer when your rank has been marked by being ineligigle for [a youth agency], or if you've been on the streets for a couple of years.

- If you've married your sweetheart, you have special honors to privacy here, you know, for fights.

- The most special members are not always the best ones; it's sometimes just the ones who have been here the first. The best ones have to wait their turn. You're not just born that easily.

- We all tried to color our hair purple to be different.

- I like the men who dress punk; they're independent.

- A piercing [for jewelry] on your face is rarely done by the weekend warriors, except for ears.

- The working girls [prostitutes] all have our hair in a long style.

- Once a girl has been pregnant, she changes, you know. She has a different feeling for life.

- The way to tell humans apart is by their shapes and the seats of their souls. It's either in the eyes or in the posture. Simply, the eyes are the keys to a person's soul. I cling to people based on their eyes. Like my soulmates here in the streets have the same eyes.

Typologizations have a traditional value of maintaining the social order of a group (Campbell, 1988). The ranking of members within the group, marked by rituals of attainment and rites of passage, strengthens the commitment to the group and its particular identity. Social isolation is the fate of any youth who has not become assimilated into and pledged fealty to a group. Further institutionalization of such social ordering is reinforced by rewarding the best performers or conformers within the group with increasing rank and social/psychological privilege.

Like in the parent culture. definitions of who is in and who is out can tighten or loosen the youths' bonds between the street culture and the draw to another culture. Advancements, in any direction, in social rank as well as age rank, are marked by ceremonies, subtle versus overt or secret versus public, and new identities, as well as some physical markers of the evolution, result. Classic markers such as permanent physical modifications of body piercing, usually for insertion of jewelry, and tattoos are overt. Clothing style can be prescribed despite the limited access to first choice clothes. Youths steal from stores and other youths because they need the popular or necessary article of clothing or accessory to complete the marker ensemble.

A fundamental deliberation of the ritual-like activities concerns the passage from the former person beyond and into the newly and socially- specifically defined and owned member. It is this common mythological process that binds both conventional and street clan groups into a social unit. Sometimes the bonds are tighter than those of blood lines. I heard one youth claim that he and a "brother" cut each other's arm and purposely mixed their blood together.

VII

Conclusions

The conceptual work in this research has located the street youths and their cultural practices in a mirrored relationship to their parent culture. My research focus is on the youths' own views and contexts for street family. Their words were framed by me to highlight their understandings and practices. These practices are functional equivalents to those of their specific family of origin, which are all embedded in the larger sociologically defined family.

I used two devices found in both cultures (family functions and mythological features) to portray the similarities between how two groups of apparently disparate people resolve basic human needs. My story line in the data analysis process is one fictive pathway that a street youth might choose. It goes something like this:

A youth who faces the loss of a functional family must make choices about how to accommodate the loss. The conditions in which the youth is making the choices are the personal bag of tricks and attributes they own and the social resources which can be accessed. The youth can choose replacement of the family or any of its component functions by recognizing the street family context. This choice is anxiety reducing.

The decision to analyze that story line, even while many other story lines await similar analysis, is in fact an act of decoding the youths' meanings and motivations. This decoding scheme claims that the youths' statements reveal their elemental human behavior as parallel to their parents' and the parent culture. Despite the youths' unconventional behaviors and lifestyle, the core cultural consciousness and beliefs match those of the parent culture's.

The findings are my interpretations of the direct quotations from the youths. It is my analysis and framing that resulted in the categories I subsequently named: loss of functional family, accommodation to the loss, gathering of tools for accommodating, replacing. and reducing anxiety. I contend that the street family is less of a physical reality and more of a reification or context for opportunities to accomplish the work described in the story line and about key categories.

The mythological features are classics, and I have done, for this culture, what mythologists do. I have interpreted what the stories mean to the psyche of the members of the culture being defined by the myths. My interpretations, here also, place the youth culture next to the parent culture.

This research depicts the social context of street youths as a restricted world with limited opportunities for interpersonal relationships. Additionally, the youths have come from dysfunctional families. They have left behind their earliest and primary experiences of family, which were abusive and neglectful relationships. They experienced an unsafe and non-nurturant environment during their developmental growth. The youths do not trust those families, other adults, or even their peers and themselves.

These barriers to developing relationships occur in a structured social context that is resource poor, threatening to health and life, and restricted in opportunities for exit out of the life. Street culture is an easily ignoble population. Street youth belong to a disenfranchised culture and have good psychological rationale to not stand up in social protest and demand equal justice.

The youths' personal networks include the adults connected to social service agencies, the tenuous ties to the family of origin, exploitive relationships within the underground economy, and other street youths. In fact, the importance of the relationships with other street youths is elevated into the institutionalization of the street fame.

Not surprisingly, these family relationships have similarities to the family of origin of the past. Understandably, beyond the fact that kinship terms and roles are borrowed, the dysfunctional model is also copied. Street family relationships are insufficient and transitory. While they appear to be intense and close, they are short lived, and the family members are interchangeable pieces. The greatest loyalty and commitment is to the concept and the idea that a family can be created and will provide safety and nurturance.

The difficulties in the lives of street youths can be survived by negotiating the physical and psychological dangers with street-specific skills. Thus, the street family as a context can be interpreted as essential to the vital, ongoing negotiation process. Program models that target street youths must respect their cultural imperatives. Street institutions must be understood in their structural and functional perspectives. Misapplied social science interventions can do more harm than simple neglect can.

It is standard among many social service workers to not speak negatively about youths' street families. This is despite a prevailing perspective that street families "enable a youth to stay in the streets." Fest (1988) points out that continued contacts with and connections into the lives of youths are his first goals.

Any supportive and long-term contact with these youths is beneficial. This population does not seek out traditional insight-oriented talk-therapy. A counseling approach that provides positive regard, respect for where the client is, and reinforcement for the youths' relationship-seeking behaviors is important. Appropriate role modeling and rewards for culturally specific positive behaviors of the youths should be provided. Any discussion about street family problems or issues is a chance for counseling the youths. Communication between a service worker and a youth seeking help is too rare an exchange. Listening to troubles or questions or just plain reports regarding the youth's street family is an excellent opportunity to display compassion and faith that the youth is worth our time.

RECOMMENDATIONS

Ending the Cycle

This study of street youth families in their subcultural contexts is a specific frame of reference of adolescents in crises. It has not hypothesized about what is normal behavior for adolescents, nor about how street youths depart from such a norm. Trying to assess what is normal and what is pathological has always been difficult. "but for the adolescent age group this seems to have been especially enigmatic" (Mitchell, 1980). Nonetheless, this study suggests questions for further study: For street youths, how is the transition from childhood to adulthood similar to or different from the transition of at-home youth? In what ways do adolescent peer groups influence social maturation? What differences exist between the peer group relationships of street youths and at-home youths?

Social service agencies and program planners could benefit from continued research into the street family context. My findings show that street families are a large piece of what keeps youths on the street or why they are so easily assimilated into the culture. This culturally stable institution is lionized by many. Alternatives to the street family context would enlarge the range of choices available to youths. Clearly, street families provide very necessary services to the youths, both to members of families and to general street culture inhabitants.

The destructive consequences of child abuse and neglect are evidenced in the increasing number of dysfunctional adolescents and adults crowding the juvenile justice and adult corrections systems. The problem of child abuse is of epidemic proportion and has been declared a national emergency year after year. Thus, one fundamental question of our era is, can the cycle of abuse of children be prevented? Anthropologically speaking, studies of high order animals reveal that abuse there is rare. Among primates studied, abusing mothers have been experimentally produced by disrupting the attachment process. The females who were prevented at birth from forming an attachment relationship with their mothers could be shown under later circumstances to be incapable of properly mothering their offspring. In some cases, the mother may even kill her infant (Krasnegar & Bridges, 1980).

Socially responsible care of children begins with an admission that our current social structures have become increasingly unkind to human life. Klantz & Pearle (1989) are clear that in modern society too much of the "natural environmental childhood" is left behind in the 20th century hunter-gatherer bands. They refer primarily to the emotional needs that are characteristically neglected in this century. Rhetorically, nobody is in favor of not giving children what they need, yet many children live in an epidemic of poverty with a chronic sense of doom. In 1993, the *Los Angeles Times* writes about government statistics of a dozen or so US children being killed every day by their parents; 13.4 million children grow up in poverty and hundreds of thousands of children are homeless. The numbers and the solutions to these national problems are complex and staggering.

Recommendations for further research include gaining an understanding of the different ways youths employ the street family context versus the ways youths use the nurturing contexts of the service structures and agencies. Additionally, there is a need for further study of the differences and similarities among the youths' patterns of dependence on and commitment to the street family contexts.

Bibliography

Adams, G., Gullotta. T., & Clancy, M. "Homeless Adolescents: A Descriptive Study of Similarities and Differences between Runaways and Throwaways." *Adolescence*, 20 (1985): 715-724.

Agar, M. H. *The Professional Sranger*. New York: Academic Press, 1980.

American Medical Association Council on Scientific Affairs. "Health Care Needs of Homeless and Runaway Youths." *JAMA: The Journal of the American Medical Association*, 262 (1989): 1358-1361.

Barden, J. C. "Homeless Youths and HIV Infection." *American Psychologist*, 46 (1990): 1188-1198.

Barrett, M., & McIntosh, M. *The Anti-social Family*. London: Verso, 1982.

Becker, H. *Sociological Work*. Chicago: Aldine, 1970.

Becker, H. & Geer, B. "Human Organization Research." In Adams & Preiss (Eds.). *Participant Observations: the Analysis of Qualitative Field Data*. Homewood, IL: The Dorsey Press, 1960.

Berman, M. *All That is Solid Melts into Air*. New York: Simon & Schuster, 1982.

Bernardes, J. "Multidimensional Developmental Pathways: A Proposal to Facilitate the Conceptualization of "Family Diversity." *Sociological Review*, 34 (1986): 590-610.

Beutler, I. F., Burr, W. R., Bahr, K. S., & Herrin, D. A. (1989). "The Family Realm: Theoretical Contributions for Understanding its Uniqueness." *Journal of Marriage and the Family*, 51 (1989): 805-816.

Blumer, H.   *Symbolic Interactionism.*   Englewood Cliffs, NJ: Prentice Hall, 1969.

Bogdan, R., & Taylor, S.   *Introduction to Qualitative Research Methods.* New York: John Wiley & Sons, Inc., 1975.

Bowlby, J. *Attachment and Loss* (Vols. 1 and 2). New York: Basic Books, 1969.

Braten, S. (1983). Quoted in Levin, I. "Family as Mapped Realities." *Journal of Family Issues*, 14 (1993).

Brooks-Gunn, J., & Furstenberg, Jr., F. "Coming of Age in the Era of AIDS: Puberty, Sexuality, and Contraception." *The Milbank Quarterly*, 68 (1990): 59-83.

Burgess, E. "The Family as a Unity of Interacting Personalities." *The Family*, (1926): 309.

—. *On Community, Family, and Delinquency.* Chicago: University of Chicago Press, 1973.

Burgess, E., & Locke, H.   *The Family: From Institution to Companionship.* New York: American Book Company, 1945.

Campbell, J. *Historical Atlas of World Mythology, Vol. II.* Cambridge: Harper and Row, 1988.

Centers for Disease Control. "HIV-related Beliefs, Knowledge, and Behaviors Among High School Students." *Morbidity and Mortality Weedly Report*, 37 (1988): 717-727.

Cheal, D. *The Gift Economy.* New York: Routledge, 1988.

—. *Family and the State of Theory.* Toronto: University of Toronto Press, 1991.

Chelimsky, E. (1982). "Homeless Youths and HIV Infection." *American Psychologist*, 46 (1982): 1188-1198.

Children's Defense Fund. "Homeless Youths and HIV Infection." *American Psychologist*, 46 (1988): 1188-1198.

Cicchetti, D., & Bughly, M. *The Self in Transition: Infancy to Childhood.* Chicago: University of Chicago Press, 1990.

Coe, Christopher L. "Psychology of Maternal Behavior in Nonhuman Primates." N.A. Krasnegor & R.S. Bridges, eds. *Mammalian Parenting.* New York: Oxford University, 1990.

Cole, P. & Putnam, F. W. (1992). "Effect of Incest on Self and Social Functioning: A Developmental Psychopathology Perspective." *Journal of Consulting and Clinical Psychology*, 60 (1992): 174-184.

Collier, J., Rosaldo, M., & Yanagisako, S. "Is There a Family?" In B. Thorne & M. Yalone (Eds.), *Rethinking the Family* (pp. 25-39). New York: Longman, 1982.

Connell, J. P. "Context, Self, and Action: A Motivational Analysis of Self Esteem Processes Across the Life Span.: In D. Cicchetti & M. Bughly (Eds.). *The Self in Transition: Infancy to Childhood.* Chicago: University of Chicago Press, 1990.

Conte, J. R., & Schuerman, J. R. "Factors Associated with an Increased Impact of Child Sexual Abuse." *Child Abuse and Neglect*, 11 (1987): 201-211.

Coyner, S. "Feminist Theory in Research and Teaching." *National Women's Studies Association*, 1 (1988-1989): 290-296.

Dalton, M. *Sociologists at Work.* Garden City, NY: Doubleday, Anchor Books, 1964.

David, E. "Sociology to Famology." *Journal of Family Issues*, 14 (1993): 20-34.

DesJarlais, D.C., & Friedman, S.R. "The Psychology of Preventing AIDS Among Intravenous Drug Users: A Social Learning Conceptualization." *American Psychologist*, 43 (1988): 865-870.

Di Clemente, R.J., Pies, C.A., Stoller, E.J., Straits, C., Olivia, G.E., Haskin, J., & Rutherford, G.W. "Evaluation of School-based AIDS Education Curricula in San Francisco." *The Journal of Sex Research*, 26 (1989): 188-198.

Downing, C. *The Goddess, Mythological Images of the Feminine.* New York: Crossroads, 1987.

Dunn, J. *The Beginnings of Social Understanding.* London: Basil Blackwell, 1988.

Edwards, J. "The Family Realm: A Future Paradigm or a Failed Nostalgia?" *Journal of Marriage and the Family*, 51 (1989): 816-818.

Egan, T. "Homeless Youths and HIV Infection." *American Psychologist*, 46 (1988): 1188-1198.

Eichler, M. "The Inadequacy of the Monolithic Model of the Family." *Canadian Journal of Sociology*, 6 (1981): 367-388.

Erikson, E. *Identity, Youth and Crisis.* New York: Norton, 1968.

Fest, J. "Street Culture and Service Delivery." In D. Boyer (ed.) *In and Out of Street Life.* Portland, OR: Tri-County Youth Services Consortium, 1988.

Flax, J. "The Family in Contemporary Feminist Thought." In J. Elshtain (ed.) *The Family in Political Thought* (pp. 223-253). Amherst: University of Massachusetts Press, 1982.

Freud, A. "Adolescence." *Psychoanalytical Study of the Child*, 13 (1958): 158-278.

Fürstenberg Jr., F., & Brooks-Gunn, J. "Teenage Childbearing: Causes, Consequences, and Remedies." In L. Arken & D. Mechanic (eds.) *Applications of Social Science to Clinical Medicine and Health Policy* (pp. 307-334). New Brunswick: Rutgers University Press, 1986.

Giddens, A. *Profiles and Critiques in Social Theory.* Berkeley: University of California Press, 1982.

Gittins, D. *The Family in Question.* Bassingstoke: Macmillan, 1985.

Glazer. N. *The Lmits of Social Policy.* Cambridge: Harvard University Press 1988.

Glantz, John K. *Exiles from Eden.* New York: W.W. Norton, 1989.

Goldscheider, F.K., & Waite, L.J. *New Families, No Families?* Berkeley: University of California Press, 1991.

Goodenough, W.H. *Cultural Anthropology and Linguistics.* Washington: Georgetown University Series, 1957.

Goodman, E., & Cohall, A.T. "Acquired Immunodeficiency Syndrome and Adolescents: Knowledge, Attitudes, Beliefs. and Behaviors in a New York City Adolescent Minority Population." *Pediatrics*, 84 (1989): 36-42.

Gubrium, J.F., & Holstein, J.A. *What is Family?* Mountain View: Mayfield, 1990.

Hammersley, M., & Atkinson, P. *Ethnography.* Cambridge: University Press, 1987.

Hampden-Turner, C. *Maps of the Mind.* New York: Macmillan, 1981.

Hartup. W.W. "Peer Relations." In E.M. Hethenngton (Ed.), *Handbook of Child Psychology: Socialization, Personality, and Development*, 4th ed. New York: Wiley, 1983.

Hein, K. "AIDS in Adolescents: Exploring the Challenge." *Journal of Adolescent Health Care*, 10 (1989): 105-355.

Hill, R. "Modern Systems Theory and the Family: A Confrontation." *Social Science Information*, 10 (1971): 7-26.

Hillman, J. *Re-Visioning Psychology*. New York: Harper and Row, 1975.

Institute of Medicine, Committee on Health Care for Homeless People. "Homeless Youths and HIV infection." *American Psychologist*, 46 (1988): 1188-1198.

James, B. *Handbook for Treatment of Attachment-Trauma Problems in Children*. New York: Lexington Books, 1994.

Josselson. R. "Ego Development in Adolescence." In J. Anderson (Ed.) *Handbook of Adolescent Psychology* (pp. 188-210). New York: Wiley, 1980.

Jung. C.G. *Jung's Collected Works*. Princeton: Princeton University Press, 1970.

Jurich. J. A. (1989). "The Family Realm: Expanding in Parameters." *Journal of Marriage and the Family*, 51 (1989): 812-821.

Kagan, J. *The Second Year: The Emergence of Self-Awareness*. Cambridge: Harvard University Press, 1981.

Katz. D. & Kahn, R.L. *The Social Psychology of Organizations*. New York: John Wiley, 1966.

Kelly. J.A., St. Lawrence, J.S., Betts, R., Brasfield, T.L., & Hood, H.W. "A Skills-Training Group Intervention Model to Assist Persons in Reducing Risk Behaviors for HIV Infection." *AIDS Education and Prevention*, 2 (1990): 24-35.

Keniston, K. "Psychological Development and Historical Change." *Journal of Interdisciplinary History*, 2 (1971).

Kopp. C.B. "Antecedents of Self-regulation: A Developmental Perspective." *Developmental Psychology*, 18 (1982): 199-214.

Landers, Ann. "Parent Poll". Summerville, J. *The Rise and Fall of Childhood*. New York: Vintage Books, 1990.

Lasch. C. *Haven in a Heartless World*. New York: Basic Books, 1977.

Levin. I. "Family as Mapped Realities." *Journal of Family Issues*, 14 (1993): 82-91.

Levitan, S.A., Belous, R.S. & Gallo, F. *What's Happening to the American Family?* Baltimore: Johns Hopkins University Press, 1988.

Liss. L. "Families and the Law." In M. B. Sussman & S.K. Steinmetz (Eds.), *Handbook of Marriage and the Family.* New York: Plenum, 1987.

Lofland, J. *Analyzing Social Settings.* Belmont: Wadsworth, 1971.

Luna. G.C. "Homeless Youths and HIV Infection." *American Psychologist,* 46 (1991): 1188-1198.

MacIntyre. S. *Single and Pregnant.* London: Croom Helm, 1977.

Main, M. & Goldwyn, R. "Predicting Rejection of her Infant from Mother's Representation of her Own Experience: Implications for the Abused-Abusing Intergenerational Cycle." *Child Abuse and Neglect,* 8 (1984): 203-217.

Mannheim K. *Ideology and Utopia.* New York: Harcourt, Brace, and World, 1966.

Mayer. R., & Greenwood. E. *The Design of Social Policy Research.* Englewood Cliffs: Prentice Hall, 1980.

Menaghan, E. G. "Escaping From the Family Realm: Reasons to Resist Claims for its Uniqueness." *Journal of Marriage and the Family.* 51 (1989): 822-825.

Mitchell, J. "Normality in Adolescence." In S. Feinstein, O. Giovacchini, J. Looney, A. Schwartzberg, & A. Gorosky (Eds.), *Adolescent Psychiatry, vol. 8;* "Developmental and Clinical Studies." Chicago: University of Chicago, 1980.

Murdock, G.P. *Social Structure.* New York: Free Press, 1949.

National Network of Runaway and Youth Services. "Homeless Youths and HIV Infection." *American Psychologist.* 46 (1991): 1188-1198.

Patton, M.Q. *Qualitative Evaluation and Research Methods.* Newbury Park: Sage Publications, 1990.

Penbridge, J.N., Yates, G.L., David, T.G., & MacKenzie, R.G. "Runaway and Homeless Youth in Los Angeles County, California." *Journal of Adolescent Health Care,* 11 (1990): 159-165.

Rapoport, R. "Ideologies about Family Forms: Towards Diversity." In K. Boh, M. Bak, C. Clason, M. Pankratona, J. Quortrup, G. Sgritta, & K. Warness (Eds.), *Changing Patterns of European Family Life* (pp. 53-69). New York: Routledge, 1989.

Robertson, M. "Homeless Youths and HIV Infection." *American Psychologist*, 46 (1989): 1188-1198.

Rotheram-Bonus, M.J., & Koopman, C. "Sexual Risk Behaviors, AIDS Knowledge, and Beliefs about AIDS Among Runaways." *American Journal of Public Health*, 81 (1991): 208-210.

Rotheram-Borus, M.J., Koopman, C., & Ehrhardt, A. "Homeless Youths and HIV Infection." *American Psychologist*, 46 (1991): 1188-1198.

Sarnoff, J. *Personality Dynamics and Development*. New York: Wiley, 1962.

Scanzoni, J. *Shaping Tomorrow's Families*. Beverly Hills: Sage, 1983. Scanzoni, J., & Marsiglio, W. "New Action Theory and Contemporary Families". *Journal of Family Issues*, 14 (1993): 105-132.

Scrimshaw, S.C., Carballo, M., Ramos, L., & Blair, B. "The AIDS Rapid Anthropological Assessment Procedures: A Tool for Health Education Planning and Evaluation." *Health Education Quarterly*, 18 (1991): 111-123.

Shaffer, D., & Caton, D. "Homeless Youths and HIV Infection." *American Psychologist*, 46 (1188-1198.

Shalwitz. J.C. Goulant, M., Dunnigan, K., & Flannery, D. "Homeless Youths and HIV Infection." *American Psychologist*, 46 (1990): 1188-1198.

Sjoberg, G. & Nett, R. *A Methodology for Social Research*. New York: Harper & Row, 1968.

Smith, D.C. *The Everyday World as Problematic: A Feminist Sociology*. Boston: Northeastern University Press, 1987.

Smith. D. "The Standard North American Family." *Journal of Family Issues*, 14 (1993): 50-65.

Sroufe, L.A., & Rutter, M. "The Domain of Developmental Psychopathology." *Child Development*, 55 (1984): 1184-1199.

Stacey, J. *Brave New Families*. New York: Basic Books, 1990.

Strauss, A., & Corbin, J. *Basics of Qualitative Research*. Newbury Park: Sage Publications, 1990.

Stricof, R., Novick, L.F., & Kennedy, J. "Homeless Youths and HIV Infection." *American Psychologist*, 46 (1991): 1188-1198.

St. Louis, M.E., Hayman, C.R., Miller, C., Anderson, J.E., Petersen, L.R., Dondero, T.J. "Homeless Youths and HIV Infection." *American Psychologist*, 46 (1989): 1188-1198.

Thomas, W.J., & Thomas, D.S. *The Child in America*. New York: Johnson Reprint, 1928.

Thome, B. "Feminist Rethinking of the Family." In B. Thorne & M. Yalom (Eds.), *Rethinking the Family*. New York: Longman, 1982.

Trost. J. "Family from a Dyadic Perspective." *Journal of Family Issues*, 14, (1993): 92- 103.

Turner, C.F., Miller, G.H., & Moses, L. E. "Homeless Youths and HIV Infection." *American Psychologist*, 46 (1989): 1188-1198.

U.S. General Accounting Office. "Homeless Youths and HIV Infection." *American Psychologist*, 46 (1989): 1188-1198.

Waters, E., Wippman, J., & Stroufe, L.A. "Attachment, Positive Affect, and Competence in the Peer Group: Two Studies in Construct Validation." *Child Development*, 50 (1979): 821-829.

Wax, M. Review of S. J. Deitchman's "The Best Laid Schemes." *Human Organization*, 37 (1977): 400-407.

Whyte, W. F. *Street Corner Society*. Chicago: University of Chicago Press, 1955.

Wilson, E.O. *On Human Nature*. Cambridge: Harvard University Press, 1978.

Yin, R.K. *Case Study Research: Design and Methods*. Beverly Hills: Sage, 1984.

Zimmerman, S. "Families as Social Systems: Implications for Family Policy." *Understanding Family Policy*. Newberry Park: Sage, 1988.

Index

Abuse, 13, 21, 52
Academic success, 48
Acceptance, 51, 31, 60
Accommodation, 40, 48
Action context, vii, xi, 17
Addicts, 21, 53
Adolescence, 21, 82
Adults, viii, 53, 55, 58
  roles of, 7
Ageist, viii
Alienation, 4, 85
Analysis, ix, 3, 57
Anger, 34
Anthropology, 14
Anxiety, 26, 39
Art, 42, 62, 73
Attachment, 84
Authenticity, 55

Beliefs, 73, 77
Betrayal, 50, 55
Bias, 27,
Bisexual youth, 25, 31, 60
Body piercing, 68

Capital, 10
Caregiver, 15, 82
Children, 64, 65
  abuse of, vii
Choice, 34
Citizens, vii
Coding, 30, 32
Communication, 61, 71
Confidentiality, 29
Contempt, viii
Context, 84
Courage, vii, xi
Culture, 6, 23
  leaders of, xii, 76
Custom, 9
Dance, 73
Decoding, 34, 81
Decompensation, 33
Democratic, 26
Demons, 66
Denial, 12
Delinquency, 4
Depression, 19
Despair, 15
Development of self, 36

Developmental psychology, 36
    of youth, 58
Deviance, xii
Dichotomy, 11, 12
Discipline, 9
Disease, 42
Disorder, 9
Displaced youth, 8, 22, 23
    tossed out, vii
Dissociation, v, 21, 22
Diversity model, 56
Divinity, 64, 72
Doom, 74
Drugs, 20
    use of, 25, 26, 45
Dysfunctional, 7, 27, 82

Economy, 3
of the underground, 72
Egalitarian relationships, 58
Emotional problems, 59, 84
Empirical realities, 82
Employment, xii, 18
Emergency shelters, 23, 42
Ethnicity, 18
Etiology, 5

Faggots, 60
Family, viii, ix
    contemporary, 7
    functional, 82
    maladaptive, x
    modern, 7
    nuclear, 11
    of origin, 81
    street, 82
    values of, xi
Famology, 11, 15, 16
Feminist perspective
    theorists, 10
Fences, 51
Foster care, 18
Freedom, 61,69,74
Friendship, 17

Frustration,
    threshold for, 4

Gay youth 76, 78
Gender, 9
Government, 51
Grounded theory, 3, 8

Harmony, 5
Health, 48
Heroes, 42, 76, 77
Heterosexuality, 31
Heterogeneity, viii
Historical benchmarks, 53
HIV infection, 11, 12,
    risk of, 24
Home, viii
Housing, 5
Hunger, 19
Hyperactivity, 33

Ideological code, 10
Incest, 4, 14
Infancy, 12
Informants, 31
Integration, 17
Interdisciplinary, viii
Interpretation, 82, 84
Interview questions, 48
Isolation, 56

Johns, 51
Justice, 82

Kinship, 9

Law, 9
    and order, vii, 68
Lesbian youth, 76
Life patterns, vii
Limitations of self,13
Loss, vii
    of functional family, 40

Malls, 37
Marginality, vii
    marginal man, 21
Marriage, 10
Maturity, 34,
Medical services, 19
Methodology, 29, 42, 83
Misrepresentation,
    deliberate, 36
Modernization, 8
Modernism,
    definition of, 12
Molestation, 43
Monopoly, 12
Myth, 63, 72, 75

Neglect, 4
New Action Theory, 18

One face, vii
Origins, 18, 37
    myths as, 42

Panhandling, 35
Parent culture, 3, 81
Patriarchy, 10, 13
Perversion, 11
Pimps, 35
Positivist, 12
Postmodern, 7, 12
Poverty, 74
Power, 63, 76
Pregnancy, 21
Prejudice, xi, 3
Production, 13
Progress, 8
Prostitution, 48
Psychopathology, 13

Quantitative, 12, 15
Qualitative research, xi, xii

Racist, viii
Ranking, 33

Rape, 51
Rationale, 29, 35
Reality, viii
Recreation, 53
Reformation, 55
Religion, 42
    as cult, 74
Replacement behavior, 31
Resources, 5
Revolutionary, xii
Ritual, 9
Runaways, 18

Sacrosanct, 74
Safety, 8
Scapegoat, viii
Scientific tradition, xi
Self-esteem, viii
Sexist, viii
Sexual Abuse, 18, 83
Sexuality, 17
Shame, 16
Social policy, viii
    responsibility, vii
    science intervention, 83
    justice, ix
    services, vii
    workers, 19
    support, xi, 19, 20
Sociology,
    imagination in, 10
Sodomy, 43
Stereotypes, viii
Story, 32
Street trash,vii
Stress, 21
    depression as, 24
Study participants, 32
Styth, 7, 8
    demographics, 3
Sugar daddies, 51
Suicide, xi
Survival, 25, 31, 38

Taxpayers, viii
Throwaways, 18
Torture, viii
Transient, 12
Trauma, 48
traumatization, 15
Tricks, 34
Two faces, vii, ix
Typology, 5

Verbalization, 5
Victims, 18, 22,
    conformity and, 68

Weapons, 67
Weekend warriors, 26
Welfare hotels, 18
Western society, 11
White, 25